Pope Leo XIV

POPE LEO XIV

Jesús Colina

Our Sunday Visitor
Huntington, Indiana

Scripture texts in this work are taken from the *New American Bible*, revised edition © 2010, 1991, 1986, 1970 Confraternity of Christian Doctrine, Washington, D.C. and are used by permission of the copyright owner. All Rights Reserved. No part of the New American Bible may be reproduced in any form without permission in writing from the copyright owner.

Excerpts from the English translation of the *Catechism of the Catholic Church* for use in the United States of America Copyright © 1994, United States Catholic Conference, Inc.—Libreria Editrice Vaticana. Used with Permission. English translation of the *Catechism of the Catholic Church*: Modifications from the Editio Typica copyright © 1997, United States Conference of Catholic Bishops—Libreria Editrice Vaticana.

Every reasonable effort has been made to determine copyright holders of excerpted materials and to secure permissions as needed. If any copyrighted materials have been inadvertently used in this work without proper credit being given in one form or another, please notify Our Sunday Visitor in writing so that future printings of this work may be corrected accordingly.

Copyright © 2025 by Jesús Colina
30 29 28 27 26 25   1 2 3 4 5 6 7 8 9

All rights reserved. With the exception of short excerpts for critical reviews, no part of this work may be reproduced or transmitted in any form or by any means whatsoever without permission from the publisher. For more information, visit: www.osv.com/permissions.

Our Sunday Visitor Publishing Division
Our Sunday Visitor, Inc.
200 Noll Plaza
Huntington, IN 46750
www.osv.com
1-800-348-2440

ISBN: 978-1-63966-229-6 (Inventory No. T2913)
1. RELIGION—Leadership.
2. RELIGION—Clergy.
3. RELIGION—Christianity—Catholic.

eISBN: 978-1-63966-230-2
LCCN: 2025938769

Cover design: Tyler Ottinger
Cover art: Vatican Media
Interior design: Amanda Falk

PRINTED IN THE UNITED STATES OF AMERICA

Contents

✠

Chapter 1: Why Has Cardinal Robert
Francis Prevost Been Elected Pope?   7

Chapter 2: Robert Francis Prevost,
the First American Pope   15

Chapter 3: A New Pope for a New World   39

Chapter 4: A Pope for the End of Christendom   51

Chapter 5: The Numbers of the Catholic Church
of Pope Leo XIV   61

Chapter 6: The Challenges Facing the
Catholic Church Today   79

Chapter 7: Signs of Hope   89

Chapter 8: Ten Messages Pope Leo XIV
Carries in His Heart   101

Epilogue: "Without Fear"   119

Notes   121

Pope Leo XIV waves to the crowd from the central balcony of St. Peter's Basilica at the Vatican as he leads, for the first time, the midday recitation of the "Regina Coeli" prayer May 11, 2025. (CNS photo/Lola Gomez, © 2025 USCCB. All rights reserved.)

Chapter 1

WHY HAS CARDINAL ROBERT FRANCIS PREVOST BEEN ELECTED POPE?

---✠---

The 69-year-old American Cardinal Robert Francis Prevost, prefect of the Vatican's Dicastery for Bishops, is the new pope, taking the name Leo XIV. Elected by the cardinals during the fourth ballot of the most recent conclave, he is now the 267th successor of Saint Peter.

The announcement of his election — using the traditional Latin formula "*Annuntio vobis gaudium magnum … Habemus Papam*" — was made by Cardinal Dominique Mamberti, Protodeacon of the College of Cardinals.

The Jubilee of Redemption 2033

The 133 cardinals elected the new pope with a very specific mission: to prepare the Barque of Peter to cross the threshold of the year 2033, a date that symbolically marks the 2000th anniversary of the passion, death, and resurrection of Jesus Christ, according to the erroneous calculations of the beginning of our era by the monk Dionysius Exiguus in the early sixth century. This event is known as the "Jubilee of the Redemption," and it will commemorate the two thousand years of the life of the Church, which began on the day of Pentecost.

The prospect of such a symbolic anniversary raised an urgent question among the participants in the Vatican conclave: Will the Catholic Church have the credibility and dynamism to present Jesus Christ as the Savior of every human being? Will the Church, and especially its pontiff, be able to propose the Gospel as the way to find the truth and happiness for which every heart longs?

We are living a disappointing paradox. On the one hand, the number of people baptized in the Catholic Church continues to grow. Humanity recently surpassed 8 billion global inhabitants,[1] of which 2.6 billion are Christians.[2] Of these, nearly 1.4 billion are baptized Catholics, according to the *Statistical Yearbook of the Church*, published by the Vatican. According to the same source, in its 2000 edition, baptized Catholics numbered just over 1 billion. Thererfore, the Church has increased 40 percent in little more than two decades.

"The Church Is Burning"

And yet, Andrea Riccardi, born in Rome in 1950, one of the most influential lay people in the Catholic Church on a global level — founder in 1968 of the Community of Sant'Egidio, one of the fastest growing Catholic movements today, professor of contemporary history at the University of Rome III, and a renowned expert on the Catholic Church in the modern and contemporary era — believes that the future of the Church itself is in danger. Riccadi wrote the Italian-language book *La Chiesa Brucia: Crisi e future del cristianesimo* (loosely translated *The Church Is Burning: Crisis and the Future of Christianity*, not yet available in English) in which he presents the fire of Notre-Dame Cathedral in Paris on April 15, 2019, as a symbol of the Church burning in the globalized world.[3] The situation of the Church today is very difficult. "Is it one of the many crises that Christianity has experienced, or is it a definitive decline?" Riccardi asks.

The crisis of meaning in the so-called Christian West is unprecedented. For the first time in history, there are countries where non-believers, agnostics, and those with no religious affiliation make up a larger proportion of the population than those who believe in an institutional religion. Recent surveys and demographic studies have shown a significant increase in the number of people who identify as having no religion, a group often referred to as the "nones."

However, a crisis does not necessarily mean the end. It can be an opportunity to be open to the future, knowing that the greater risk is to be content with merely surviving, longing for a better past. The most important struggle for the Church at this time, Riccardi says, is not against external enemies, but against internal divisions and external indifference and discredit.

Finally, Riccardi leaves the floor to Fr. Alexander Vladimirovich Men, a Soviet Russian Orthodox priest, harrassed by the KGB, and possibly a victim of the KGB in 1990, who wrote:

> Only short-sighted people imagine that Christianity has already happened, that it took place, say, in the thirteenth century, or the fourth, or some other time. I would say that it has only made the first hesitant steps in the history of the human race. Many words of Christ are incomprehensible to us even now, because we are still Neanderthals in spirit and morals; because the arrow of the Gospels is aimed at eternity; because the history of Christianity is only beginning. What has happened already, what we now call the history of Christianity, are the first half-clumsy, unsuccessful attempts to make it a reality.[4]

As they secluded themselves in the Sistine Chapel (before Michelangelo's *Last Judgment* fresco) to participate in the voting that elected Cardinal Prevost, this reality must surely have been revolving in the minds and hearts of the cardinal electors. The conclave was preceded by the so-called general congregations, meetings in which all cardinals, including those who could not participate in the conclave because they were over eighty years old, discussed the historical challenge facing the Catholic Church and the profile that the new Bishop of Rome should have.

Soon the gaze of the cardinals, with their purple-red cassocks, a symbol of their willingness to be faithful to the pope and to defend the Church to the last drop of their blood — that is, to martyrdom — settled on the Robert Francis Prevost. Although they had not had many opportunities to meet and get to know one another, his figure gradually became a symbol of hope.

They paid attention to the sparkle in his eyes and, above all, to his serene, unforced smile. They consulted his biography, and what stood out to them was not only his ability to advise the pope in the selection and governance of bishops around the world, but his missionary spirit. They saw a son of Saint Augustine capable of inspiring love. They did not need many exchanges. These successors of the apostles concluded that he was the man called to lead the Church, as the apostle Peter did in the early years of Christianity (see Mt 16:18–19).

Why Cardinal Prevost Was Elected Pope

The electoral process of the conclave is characterized by absolute secrecy. The apostolic constitution *Universi Dominici Gregis*, promulgated by Pope St. John Paul II on February 22, 1996, the feast of the Chair of Peter, and subsequent changes introduced by his successors, impose severe sanctions on any cardinal (or other person involved) who violates the oath of secrecy regarding the procedures or discussions that take place within the conclave. These sanctions may include excommunication, which is one of the most serious penalties in the Catholic Church and means that the individual is excluded from communion with the Church and from the sacraments.

The secrecy of the conclave is intended to protect the freedom and independence of the cardinals in their election, ensuring that their decision is based solely on their consideration of who is the best candidate to be the next pope, without outside influence or pressure. Secrecy also helps to preserve the dignity of the process and of the cardinals involved by avoiding public speculation and judgment about the deliberations and voting.

The secrecy makes the work of journalists particularly difficult, however. Moreover, if the journalist is a Catholic believer, he or she is implicated in this process, which, if not respected, can also lead to excommunication. However, based on conversations with the cardinals and press reports published after the conclave, we can say that there are several obvious reasons that led the cardinals to target Robert Francis Prevost.

The election of Leo XIV was, above all, a surprise, primarily because of the name of the chosen candidate, who was not among the top preferences on the lists of *papabile* published by journalists in the days leading up to the vote. It was also surprising for the speed of the election: Only four ballots were needed to reach the two-thirds majority — at least eighty-nine votes.

The pre-conclave general congregations of all the cardinals, including those over the age of eighty who were not eligible to vote, were striking for the clarity with which the challenges facing the Church were presented. Some even considered the tone of the discussions to be quite severe.

In the general congregations before the previous conclave, the urgent need had been identified to choose a pope capable of advancing the reform of the Roman Curia, which had been shaken by scandals — most notably, the so-called Vatileaks. The cardinals at that time chose Jorge Mario Bergoglio.

In this conclave, regardless of whether a cardinal was considered "conservative" or "progressive," there was broad agreement that one of the greatest challenges facing the Church today is unity — unity in a world threatened by the hatred of polarization, unity in a Church suffering from deep internal divisions.

Prevost's profile soon emerged as that of the man for the moment. An American and the son of immigrants, he embodied the example of a missionary who leaves everything behind to dedicate himself to God and to his brothers and sisters in a distant land — in his case, Peru. A man of proven leadership, he had served as the superior of one of the Church's most prominent religious orders, the Augustinians. In recent years, he had been entrusted with one of the pope's most challenging responsibilities: proposing candidates for the episcopate around the world. Most of the cardinals knew him, as they had had the opportunity to deal with him in their important positions.

This role of Prevost seems to have contributed to the cardinal electors viewing him as a man of unity. His first words as pope, from the balcony of St. Peter's Basilica in the Vatican, were devoted to unity — to a Church "that always seeks peace, that always seeks charity."

An Intriguing Question: Divine Inspiration?

This reasoning leads to an intriguing question for a journalist who considers himself a believer: How is it possible to reconcile the agreements, deliberations, negotiations, and even "alliances" among cardinals inherent in any process of electing a representative with the Church's openly proclaimed conviction that this process is guided by the inspiration of the Holy Spirit?

In Christianity, the religion of the incarnate God, there can be no contradiction between faith and reason. When it becomes clear to the College of Cardinals that a candidate has the most appropriate qualities to lead the Church at a particular moment in history, everyone assumes that this shared clarity is part of the discernment process, and therefore the fruit of divine inspiration.

This happened in AD 50 during the Council of Jerusalem, described in Acts 15, which set a precedent for Church decision-making and the handling of doctrinal disputes. At issue was the question of whether Gentiles who converted to Christianity had to follow Jewish practices, especially circumcision, in order to be saved. The meeting included the apostles and elders, as well as the general fellowship. There was much discussion, allowing different parties to express their views. Peter, Paul, and Barnabas presented their personal views. James quoted Scripture to support the inclusion of the Gentiles and presented a solution that did not require circumcision of Gentile converts, but did require them to abstain from certain practices associated with idolatry. James' proposal was accepted.

This first council established a model for resolving conflict and making doctrinal decisions within the Church through dialogue, consultation, and consensus; and it emphasized the central role of Scripture and the guidance of the Holy Spirit in the Church's decision-making.

Something similar happened in the Sistine Chapel during this most recent conclave. Without this perspective, it is very difficult to understand the nature of a conclave, and even less the nature of the Catholic Church itself. For the nearly 5,000 journalists from all continents who covered the conclave, the election process became one of the most exotic events in world news: elderly gentlemen, lifelong celibates, dressed in ancient costumes and vibrant colors, gathered in the smallest state in the world, surrounded by works of art that have marked the history of humanity. For many journalists, it was like writing the chronicle of a soccer match without knowing the rules of the game. In the end, trying to explain what happened, as in any other political election, everything ends up being judged in terms of the political categories we are all used to: liberal and conservative, left and right, traditionalist and modernist. Yet the reality is that Christianity adds an intangible factor to the conclave that changes everything: the conviction that in the fragility of those men gathered to choose the successor of Peter, God is writing history with what appears to us as crooked lines.

This can be better understood with the help of an anecdote widely circulated in Rome, the original source of which I have not been able to verify. It directly concerns Ludwig von Pastor (1854–1928), a German historian, naturalized Austrian, author of the monumental *History of the Popes from the Close of the Middle Ages* (*Geschichte der Päpste seit dem Ausgang des Mittelalters*), published in forty volumes in its original German between 1886 and 1933, the last volume, posthumously. An acquaintance once asked von Pastor why he had converted to Catholicism and remained a Catholic when, as a historian, he was acutely aware of the frequent bad habits of popes, cardinals, bishops, and pastors of the Church. That the Church was still standing after so much time, despite the misdeeds of some of its pastors, the historian replied, meant the Church really was and is a work of God.

This book offers the reader a most exciting journey: On the one hand, we will discover the enormous challenges that have led qualified observers to believe that the Catholic Church could collapse in the not too distant future. On the other hand, we will discover how life, spirituality, and leadership have prepared Cardinal Robert Francis Prevost to become the new successor of Saint Peter. We will discover hidden signs of hope. And we will understand why martyrs like Alexander Men thought that the adventure of Christianity has only just begun.

Chapter 2

ROBERT FRANCIS PREVOST, THE FIRST AMERICAN POPE

─────────────✠─────────────

It's a day like any other in 1961. The scene takes place in a simple brick house in Dolton, a suburb south of Chicago. Inside, three young children, three brothers, are playing. You hear, "Stop, you're under arrest!" The two older boys, Louis and John, are running around the house, playing cops and robbers. Their mother, Mildred, calls out to them in a gentle voice, as she has done so many times before, "Be careful with the ironing board!"

Something special is happening on this ironing board. The youngest brother, Robert, age six, is standing there. His concentration indicates that something very important is happening: He is reciting

Childhood home of Robert Prevost, now Pope Leo XIV, in Dolton, Illinois. (Michael Howie/Wikimedia Commons)

the words of the Eucharistic consecration. It is almost time for "Communion."

Louis and John, having heard their mother, come over to see what their little brother is doing. Rob, as he is called by his brothers, shows them a wafer, which he has taken out of a Necco tube, as if it were a consecrated host. Louis and John receive "Communion." Their mother watches the scene and calls everyone to the table; it is time for lunch. Their father, Louis, looks up with a smile from the book he is reading.

The Call

"Rob, one day you'll be pope in Rome!" says the older brother, Louis, jokingly to his little brother. No one could have imagined that Louis had prophetic gifts. In the 1960s, the last time the Church had had a non-Italian pope was in 1523, when the Dutch Adrian VI was elected. To think that an American boy — a fan of the Chicago White Sox — could one day become pope seemed unreal. But Louis was not the only one to say so; one of the neighbors, admiring little Robert's religiosity in church, had already mentioned it. A first-grade classmate also teased him about it. In reality, they were simply noting that this child deeply believed in what he wanted to be when he grew up: a priest.

Now, in 2025, how was it possible for the conclave to elect an American pope, something totally unimaginable just over sixty years ago? The man's biography is the best answer.

Robert Francis Prevost was born in Chicago September 14, 1955. His mother, Chicago-born Mildred Agnes Martínez, of Spanish and Creole origin, had followed an exceptional academic path for that time in history. She earned a bachelor's degree in education in 1947 and pursued graduate studies in library science at DePaul University. She worked as a school librarian and later became the librarian at Chicago's cathedral.

She was one of the driving forces behind the local parish, St. Mary of the Assumption, where she was active in the Altar and Rosary Society. She loved to sing and was very talented, which she expressed above all in the parish choir. She also enjoyed preparing and participating in parish school plays. She had her three children in just four years.

In his first Sunday address as pope, Leo XIV implicitly remembered her on May 11, 2025, congratulating all mothers — including those who are already in heaven — with emotion. Mildred Prevost died in 1990, after being diagnosed with cancer and undergoing chemotherapy.

Pope Leo's father, Louis Marius, several years younger than his wife, was of French-Italian descent and an educator by vocation. He worked as superintendent of Brookwood School District 167 in Glenwood, Illinois; as principal of Mount Carmel Elementary School, a Catholic school in Chicago Heights; and as superintendent of the southern suburban schools in District 169.

Before that, he served in the United States Navy during World War II. Commissioned in November 1943, he served as the executive officer of a tank-landing ship and took part in the D-Day landings in

Normandy, France, in June 1944.

Like his wife, Louis also devoted most of his free time to his children and the parish, where he was a catechist. He died in 1997. His sons' professions testify to how their father inspired their lives: Louis joined the US Navy, as his father had done; John devoted his life to education, becoming a Catholic school principal, like his father.

All three brothers studied at the parish school. It was in this close-knit family environment that Robert Prevost discovered his calling to become a priest, as he himself revealed a few weeks before being elected pope in an interview with RAI, the Italian public television channel. At that time, he did not yet know how or where he would be able to consecrate himself to God. Life would show him the way.

Farewell to the Family, Entry into the Minor Seminary

As he entered adolescence, Robert continued to cultivate his desire to become a priest. However, something unexpected happened, which was a surprise even to his parents. Against the advice of his parish priest, Robert decided not to enter the seminary of the Archdiocese of Chicago.

He knew other boys who had entered the minor seminary of the Augustinian religious order, and he was attracted to it. "I made up my mind. All right, I thought. I'll enter this seminary. And then we'll see," Prevost recalled in that interview with RAI.[5] "I entered as a boy at the age of fourteen, and what came next was history."

Despite their surprise, his mother and father supported his decision. In the summer of 1969, Robert said good-bye to them and his two brothers, left home, and went to study at St. Augustine Seminary High School in Holland, Michigan.

The decision to enter the Augustinian seminary would change his life forever. There, in the midst of adolescence, he came into contact with someone who would be present in his daily life as a friend and advisor: St. Augustine of Hippo. Discovering one of the greatest theologians, philosophers, and saints in history during his adolescence would definitively shape his way of thinking and his Christian identity.

Undated picture of Robert Prevost. (Photo Courtesy of the Midwest Augustinian Province of Our Mother of Good Counsel)

"As a young man living with other young people, those were years of self-discovery, which was also important as a son of Saint Augustine," Prevost recalled. "They were years of getting to know others and seeing the importance of friendship and community life." Fr. Becket Franks, OSB, a Benedictine monk at St. Procopius Abbey in Lisle,

Illinois, and a seminary classmate who was a year ahead of him, recalls that all the students knew each other at that school, as there were no more than sixty-five students. "I was in choir with Bob. I was in the reader's theater with him. We interacted all the time together," recalls the Benedictine. "The most outstanding thing is how smart he is. He was into everything, he knew everything, and it came easily. And he brought all of us along with him." Father Franks also remembers: "He was known as the tutor of the school; if you had problems with your English paper, go see Prevost. If you had problems with your math homework, go see Prevost. If you didn't understand some history project, go see Bob. And Bob would help us."[6]

During his time at the seminary, Prevost stood out both for his academic excellence and his leadership skills. He was editor in chief of the school yearbook, vice president of the student council, and president of his class his senior year.

After completing minor seminary in 1973, Robert kept alive the flame of the priestly vocation he had received in childhood. He entered Villanova University in Pennsylvania, an institution of the Augustinian order, to study mathematics and philosophy.

Augustinian Fr. Peter M. Donohue, president of Villanova University since 2006, explains that Robert was in a period of formation and discernment while at Villanova. Father Donohue explains this as "a period of examining and looking at what it is, and do you want to live this life, but you're not in vows or anything."[7]

Robert lived in the St. Mary's Hall dormitory on campus. In addition to studying for two degrees, he was involved in student life, co-founding the university organization Villanovans for Life, committed to defending the right to life of the unborn.

He earned his bachelor's degree in math in 1977. Robert, who had also studied philosophy at Villanova, was well aware of his human and intellectual abilities, and he knew he could pursue a successful and lucrative professional career. However, he remained faithful to the calling he had experienced since childhood. "In those years, a certain restlessness grew in me, a desire to be a missionary — that is, not to stay in my own country, but to participate in some way in another type of work as a priest, as a religious," he explained in his interview with RAI.

Like everyone else, he also had moments of doubt and crisis. When he experienced them, Prevost recalls:

> I had confidence in my parents. The family was very close … I talked to my father, but not as if he were a spiritual director. We talked about very concrete things, about the doubts that a young man can feel when he thinks: "Maybe it's better to give it up. I'll leave this life and get married. I want to have children. I want a normal life, like the one I knew through my family."… My father, with his experience, talked about life, about the intimacy between him and my mother and how important it was. And at the same time, he told me how important it is in the life of a vocation to the priesthood to be close to Christ, to know Jesus, to truly know the love of God in your life. Although these were things I had heard a hundred times from my formators and other priests, when my father spoke to me in this way, in a very human but very profound way, I said to myself, "I have to listen."[8]

Son of Saint Augustine

On September 1, 1977, Robert entered the novitiate of the Order of St. Augustine in St. Louis, part of the Augustinian Province of Our Mother of Good Counsel. As a novice, he lived in community with other young people and Augustinian religious, experiencing firsthand the fundamental values of the Order of St. Augustine.

One of the primary values of this religious order is interiority. Augustinian spirituality emphasizes the search for God within the human being. It is an invitation to deep introspection to find the truth and the divine presence in the heart of each person. This interiority is cultivated through prayer, contemplation, and study, promoting an intimate relationship with God.

In the novitiate, Robert also discovered the importance of community life. The members of the Order of St. Augustine live with "one soul and one heart directed toward God," as Saint Augustine desired, sharing material and spiritual goods. In community, Robert grew to understand the meaning of the apostolic service that Augustinians offer to the world and to the Church through the works and missions they animate and direct.

It was a year of reading, meditating, and delving deeper into the author who would become his spiritual father: Saint Augustine. Robert was amazed with every page he read. In the writings of the saint from North Africa, he discovered new recesses of his own soul. He learned Latin to better understand the original writings of this great Doctor of the Church. Although Augustine had died in 430, his *Confessions, City of God*, and his sermons resonated in Robert's heart as if they had just been written.

At the end of his year at the novitiate, Robert made his first profession of vows of poverty, chastity, and obedience according to the rule and constitutions of the Order of St. Augustine on September 2, 1978. He thus became, as his habit showed, a son of Augustine.

Theological Formation and Solemn Profession

Robert's path to priesthood continued that year with theological studies. This meant returning to his native Chicago to study at the Catholic Theological Union (CTU), an academic institution made up of various religious orders, where he obtained a Master of Divinity degree in 1982.

During this period, he also taught mathematics and physics at St. Rita of Cascia Catholic High School in Chicago and occasionally assisted at St. Gabriel Parish in the Canaryville neighborhood, where his brother John was principal of the elementary school.

The pastoral focus of the formation provided by the CTU confirmed his vocation as a missionary, which became increasingly clear in his heart.

Prevost's vision of the Church, which he himself expresses in his interview with RAI, stems from his theological formation:

I think that today the voice of the Church, not of the institution, but of the Church lived as a communion of the faithful, with the martyrs, with the presence and witness of women and men who give their lives even in situations of violence and war, is a voice that offers great hope to the world. Unfortunately, not everyone wants to hear the message. This is a great challenge for the Church. Too often we have allowed the Church to become an institution. There are institutional dimensions, but that is not the heart that the Church should have.[9]

As he neared the end of his theology studies in Chicago, near the feast day of St. Augustine of Hippo, Robert experienced one of the most anticipated days of his life. Three years after his first profession, he solemnly — that is, perpetually — pronounced his vows of poverty, chastity, and obedience on August 29, 1981. He thus became a full member of the Order of St. Augustine. This implied total belonging to the religious community, sharing its life, prayer, apostolate, and goods in common. Robert Francis Prevost added three letters after his name: OSA, meaning Order of Saint Augustine.

Ordination to the Priesthood and Studies in Rome

After finishing the academic year in 1982, Robert prepared for what he thought would be the most important day of his life: ordination to the priesthood. However, his superiors added a new challenge. He had proven himself to be highly intelligent and capable, and now he was being asked to go to Rome to specialize in canon law, the legal regulations of the Catholic Church. It was very important for the order to have among its members, particularly since some would become its future superiors, experts capable of ensuring that the provisions of religious government respected the legal order of the Church.

He was offered the opportunity to pursue this specialization at an institution with one of the most prestigious faculties in the Catholic world, the Pontifical University of St. Thomas Aquinas, better known as the Angelicum, run by the Order of Preachers, the Dominicans.

So, Robert Prevost, not yet twenty-seven years old, received the

Sacrament of Holy Orders on June 19, 1982, in the Eternal City, in the chapel of the Augustinian College of St. Monica. He was ordained by Belgian Archbishop Jean Jadot (1909–2009), who was then responsible for the Vatican's Secretariat for Non-Believers, and who until shortly before had been the pope's representative (apostolic delegate) in the United States.

Father Prevost spent his first two years as a priest in Rome, completing his licentiate in canon law in 1984. This was an opportunity to learn to speak Italian well, which would be decisive for the successful performance of his future responsibilities as a superior in the Augustinian order as well as for the Church in general.

After completing his degree, his superiors felt that his years of study were not yet over. They encouraged him to continue his academic training in order to prepare a doctoral thesis in canon law.

However, Father Robert's missionary heart was beating fast. His superiors knew this. Therefore, in 1985, they proposed that he respond to the needs of the order in Peru and he would be sent to the Augustinian mission in Chulucanas. Obviously, the condition was that he had to continue studying to complete his doctorate.

He fulfilled his commitment and, sacrificing sleep and finding time wherever he could, two years later was able to defend his doctoral thesis, "The Role of the Local Prior in the Order of Saint Augustine," a detailed canonical analysis of more than four hundred pages on the internal government of the Augustinian order, specifically examining the responsibilities and authority of the local superior. The thesis still represents a contribution of particular interest to Augustinian studies and to the field of canon law relating to institutes of consecrated life.

What Father Prevost could never have imagined was that this solid academic training in canon law, with a specialization in religious governance, would prove invaluable after his election as pope, since his pontificate has, among other challenges, the task of structuring reforms introduced by Pope Francis in accordance with canon law.

Missionary in Peru

When he landed in Peru, Father Robert was fulfilling a dream. "I felt

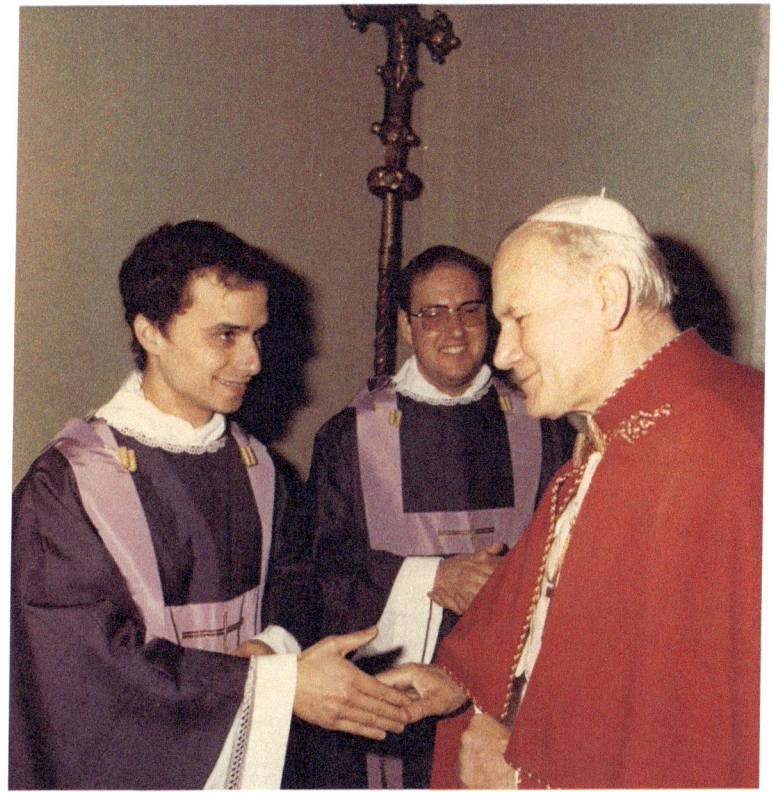

Undated picture of Robert Prevost with Pope John Paul II. (Photo Courtesy of the Midwest Augustinian Province of Our Mother of Good Counsel)

the desire to be a missionary, not to stay in my country. I wanted to participate, in some way, in something bigger," he explained in his interview with RAI.

During his first mission in Peru, between 1985 and 1986, he served as parish vicar of the cathedral and chancellor of the Territorial Prelature of Chulucanas. Today, this ecclesiastical district (now a diocese) has a population of 479,000, of whom 85 percent are Catholic. It is located in the Piura region of Peru, embracing regions as diverse as the Sechura Desert and the foothills of the Andes.

Chulucanas has a deep Augustinian missionary heritage. In 1962, Pope St. John XXIII asked religious orders in the United States to send 10 percent of their members to evangelize Latin America. He later specifically invited the Augustinians of the Midwest Province of Our Mother of Good Counsel to care for missionary territory in northern Peru. The Augustinians accepted and began their missionary service in 1964. Their primary assignment was to the newly created Prelature of Chulucanas.

The pastoral work of these religious laid the foundation for the growth of the local Church and the formation of native clergy, to the point that in 1988, shortly after Father Prevost's arrival, Pope St. John Paul II elevated the territory to the rank of diocese. Today, pastoral work is carried out through twenty-two parishes, a hospital, and a Catholic university distributed throughout the diocese.[10]

In that first missionary experience in Peru, Fr. Robert Prevost collaborated closely with the bishop prelate in the pastoral organization of a largely rural area with a shortage of clergy. He learned the Spanish language and sought to understand popular religiosity and Peruvian culture, integrating himself with simplicity into the life of the communities where he served.

In 1987, after defending his doctoral thesis, he took up the position of director of vocations and missions for the Augustinian Province of Our Mother of Good Counsel in Chicago. He also worked for a time with the faculty of the Augustinian Novitiate in Oconomowoc, Wisconsin, before returning to Peru.

In 1988 he was sent to the city of Trujillo, where the Augustinians had another important mission. There, Father Prevost carried out intense pastoral and formative work for a decade (1988–98), carefully fulfilling multiple responsibilities. During this time, he served as prior — that is, local superior of his Augustinian religious brothers — of the Augustinian community in Trujillo (1988–92), director of formation for Augustinian aspirants (1988–98), and later master of professed (religious formation director, from 1992 to 1998).

He harmonized these responsibilities with other important positions in the service of the Archdiocese of Trujillo. He was judicial vicar (1989–98), serving in the local ecclesiastical court, where he applied his knowledge of canon law in the service of the Peruvian Church. He was also professor of canon law, patristics, and moral theology at the

San Carlos y San Marcelo Major Seminary in Trujillo, forming future priests.

In addition, Father Robert served poor communities on the outskirts of Trujillo, taking charge of the chaplaincy of Nuestra Señora Madre de la Iglesia (1988–99), a mission that would later become Santa Rita Parish. He was also parish administrator of Nuestra Señora de Montserrat (1992–99), closely accompanying the faithful in humble neighborhoods.

This intense missionary experience was extremely enriching for Father Prevost, as he recalled in his interview with RAI. "There I matured in my experience as a religious," he said. "I discovered the value of closeness, of life among the people, and of mission as a silent but concrete witness."

Superior of the Augustinians

After these ten years of mission, Robert Prevost was called to assume greater responsibilities in the government of his order. His Augustinian brothers valued his calm leadership and international experience. Thus, in 1999, he was elected provincial prior of the Order of St. Augustine's Province of Our Mother of Good Counsel in Chicago, his home province.

This put him at the head of the Augustinian communities in the Midwest region of the United States, but it was to be a brief period; barely two years later, in 2001, during the ordinary general chapter of the Order of St. Augustine, Father Prevost was elected prior general. He thus became the superior general of all 2,888 Augustinian religious and novices in the world at that time, including 2,168 priests distributed across five continents in 465 communities.[11]

The order traces its origins back to Saint Augustine himself, who, after his conversion, gathered his friends to serve God, organizing their life according to the ideal of the Acts of the Apostles. Augustine first settled in the city of Tagaste as a layman and then, after he became a priest, in Hippo. He wrote a rule of life that his communities followed.

After Augustine's death in 430, barbarians invaded North Afri-

Undated picture of Robert Prevost with Pope Benedict XVI. (Photo Courtesy of the Midwest Augustinian Province of Our Mother of Good Counsel)

ca, and the Roman Empire fell. Members of the communities fled persecution and settled in regions of Europe. These small communities lived for centuries as hermits, following the Augustinian rule and spirit.

In 1244, these communities were summoned by Pope Innocent IV and gathered together, thus beginning the history of the order. Twelve years later, Pope Alexander IV promoted what is known as the "Great Union." This papal act integrated other groups of hermits who had not joined in 1244. In this way, the Augustinian ideal spread, giving impetus to the order, which eventually expanded to the Americas, Asia, and back to Africa, its land of origin.

Upon becoming prior general of the Order of St. Augustine, Father Prevost took up residence at the Pontifical Augustinian Institute, located next to St. Peter's Square in the Vatican. The missionary and international dimension that had characterized Father Prevost's career was also evident in his governance as prior general. He traveled constantly, visiting Augustinian communities on different continents, strengthening unity, and encouraging the pastoral and social work of the order in very diverse contexts.

His first term was from 2001 to 2007. After this period, the delegates of the order ratified their confidence in him and reelected him for a second term. In total, he served twelve years as prior general (2001–13).

During his term, he promoted Augustinian formation and studies and was responsible for the order's relations with the Vatican dicasteries. He was also responsible for dealing with many of the issues that arose between the order and bishops around the world.

His approachable and humble manner, combined with a solid analytical ability — in part inherited from his academic training — enabled him to govern the Order of St. Augustine with a spirit of deep listening, but at the same time with firmness and a spirit of service, earning the appreciation of his religious brothers.

Under his guidance through the first years of the new millennium, the order faced challenges such as the decline in vocations in some countries and missionary expansion in others. Through it all, Prevost promoted the vision of a Church that was close to the people, encouraging his friars to be present among those most in need, just as he himself had lived in Peru.

One of his significant achievements was the return of the Augustinian presence to Cuba. After a meeting in 2005 with Cuban bishops, including Cardinal Jaime Ortega, steps were taken to reestablish the order on the island, which had been absent since 1961. This came to fruition in 2006 with the arrival of Augustinian religious.

Robert Prevost concluded his second term as prior general September 4, 2013, after having exhausted the maximum term of office allowed by the order's constitutions. In October 2013, he returned to

Chicago where he filled several roles: director of formation at St. Augustine's Convent, first counselor, and provincial vicar.

Missionary Bishop in Peru

A year later, something unexpected happened. On November 3, 2014, Pope Francis appointed him apostolic administrator of the Peruvian diocese of Chiclayo. He entered the diocese on November 7, in the presence of the apostolic nuncio, Archbishop James Patrick Green, who ordained him bishop a little over a month later, on December 12, the feast of Our Lady of Guadalupe, in the Cathedral of Santa María.

In a video recorded in a Franciscan community on March 14, 2023, Bishop Prevost recounted what his relationship with Pope Francis was like at that time:

> I knew Jorge Mario Bergoglio, archbishop of Buenos Aires at the time, when I was general of the Augustinians. We had met several times. When he was elected pope, I said to some of my brothers, "Well, that's very good, thank God I'll never be a bishop." I'm not going to tell you the reason, but let's just say that not in all my meetings with Cardinal Bergoglio were we always in agreement. Then I invited him to preside over the opening Mass of the Augustinian General Chapter on August 28, 2013. Everyone had told me, "The pope has never done that." But he accepted. And he presided over the Mass in St. Augustine's Church, where Saint Monica's tomb is located. When he visited Rome as cardinal, he always stopped by the tomb of Saint Monica. On this occasion, at the end of Mass, he said to me, "Now rest in your country." He left me for a few months and then appointed me bishop. I don't know when the rest will come, but here we are.

In his first year as bishop, Prevost requested and obtained Peruvian citizenship, further strengthening his ties to the country. During his time in Chiclayo, he was recognized for his simple and direct pastoral style, his closeness to the people, and his clear preference for the poor and most vulnerable.

One of the phenomena that tested his leadership was the El Niño Costero event in 2017, which caused severe flooding in the region. Bishop Prevost stood out for his immediate and practical response, mobilizing the Church to bring humanitarian aid to the affected communities, even participating himself in the distribution of basic necessities and food in areas that were difficult to access. He is remembered for being "in boots and a poncho" in the mud, accompanying those who suffered losses.

Later, during the COVID-19 pandemic, the diocese, under his leadership, promoted the Oxygen of Hope campaign, a crucial initiative to make available medical oxygen equipment in response to desperate need and the collapse of the healthcare system, saving numerous lives in the region.

A photo went around the world showing the bishop, dressed in liturgical vestments, carrying the Eucharist in a monstrance in procession through the streets of Chiclayo, offering hope to people who came to their windows to see him pass by.

In addition to his response to emergencies, Bishop Prevost was concerned with the pastoral organization of the diocese, encouraging active participation of the laity and relying on various ecclesial organizations for formation and pastoral work. His knowledge of canon law was also an asset to the diocese. He also showed interest in issues such as integral ecology, creating a specific diocesan commission.

His work spread throughout Peru. In March 2018, he was elected second vice president of the Peruvian Episcopal Conference, within which he was also a member of the Economic Council and president of the Culture and Education Commission.

In April 2022, three women filed complaints against two priests of the Diocese of Chiclayo, alleging that they had been victims of sexual abuse when they were minors. The complainants claimed that, despite having informed then-Bishop Prevost, no adequate measures were taken to investigate the cases. In response to these allegations, the Diocese of Chiclayo issued a statement on September 10, 2024, denying any attempt at a cover-up by Prevost.

Pope Francis gives the red biretta to new Cardinal Robert F. Prevost during the September 30, 2023 consistory. (Photo CNS/Lola Gomez, © 2023 USCCB. All rights reserved.)

According to the statement, precautionary measures were taken against the priests involved, and the case was referred to the Dicastery for the Doctrine of the Faith in July 2022. The case was closed in August 2023 because the alleged acts had already been time-barred.

The current bishop of Chiclayo, Edinson Farfán, OSA, publicly defended his predecessor, stating that Prevost "respected the internal procedures" of the Church in cases of sexual assault and that he "listened to and accompanied the victims." Bishop Farfán also stressed that a distinction must be made between the canonical process and the civil process, and that the Church is caring for the women who suffered the abuse.

On January 30, 2023, Pope Francis surprised everyone by calling Prevost from his remote Peruvian bishopric to appoint him to one of the most senior positions in the Church, prefect of the Dicastery for Bishops. This mission involves assisting the pontiff in the selection of bishops around the world. The position also involved being president of the Pontifical Commission for Latin America.

In the previously mentioned video recorded March 2023, Bishop Prevost summed up his experience as bishop of Chiclayo: "Those eight years have been a time of great formation, personal education, a great treasure. I am truly torn. The pope knows this, too. My preference would have been to remain in Chiclayo, but one must obey at all stages of life. And once again, I thank Pope Francis for this great show of confidence in me."

Working with Francis

A new experience began for Robert Prevost in Rome, as he accepted many new responsibilities. On September 30, 2023, Pope Francis made him a cardinal and assigned him the Diaconate of Saint Monica. As head of the Dicastery for Bishops, Cardinal Prevost participated in the pope's apostolic journeys and in both sessions of the Synod of Bishops on Synodality (October 4–29, 2023, and October 2–27, 2024).

Pope Francis also appointed Cardinal Prevost as a member of the Dicasteries for Evangelization, for the Doctrine of the Faith, for the Eastern Churches, for the Clergy, for Institutes of Consecrated Life and Societies of Apostolic Life, for Culture and Education, for Legislative Texts, and of the Pontifical Commission for Vatican City State.[12]

For Cardinal Prevost, amid so many responsibilities, one of the most motivating moments was the regular meeting he had every Saturday morning, for two years, with Francis to discuss issues related to the Dicastery for Bishops.

"Until the end, [Pope Francis] wanted to give everything for his ministry, for his work, for his service to the Church," Cardinal Prevost explained in an interview with *Vatican News* after Francis's death.[13]

"At first it was at 8 a.m. But sometimes I would arrive at 7:30, and he was already waiting for me, so I started going a little earlier, and sometimes he would arrive early." Important issues were discussed, but Francis would often add a recommendation: "He would say to me, among other things, at the end of the audience: 'Don't lose your sense of humor, you have to smile.'"

Cardinal Prevost played a prominent role in the two sessions of the Synod on Synodality. His role as prefect of the Dicastery for Bishops since 2023 was particularly influential in discussions on the structure of the Church and the exercise of the episcopal ministry in a synodal context.

He was a strong promoter of synodality, understanding it not as the promotion of a political agenda, but as a process of listening to the Holy Spirit and "walking together" as the People of God. He emphasized the importance of overcoming polarization and promoting a more inclusive and participatory Church at all levels.

On several occasions, Cardinal Prevost has linked synodality to the roots of the early Church and to the teachings of the Second Vatican Council, presenting this synodal path as a necessary renewal for the Church's evangelizing mission in today's world.

In a speech to journalists on October 23, 2024, within the context of the Synod on Synodality, he illustrated the need for a more synodal process of selecting bishops, seeking greater participation of the "People of God," which includes not only bishops and priests, but also religious and laity.

He stressed the importance of apostolic nuncios, who are responsible for gathering information on candidates for the episcopate, having a detailed knowledge of the local reality and listening to the faithful in order to identify pastors who will have the "smell of the sheep" — who are close to their people and willing to walk and suffer with them, not merely serving as administrators.

Regarding the role of women in the Church, Cardinal Prevost, in a press conference given in the context of the Synod on Synodality on October 25, 2023, maintained a position in line with traditional doctrine on the non-ordination of women to the priesthood. He noted

Pope Leo XIV (then-Cardinal Robert F. Prevost, OSA) celebrates Mass at St. Jude Parish in New Lenox, Illinois, in 2024. (Photo Courtesy of the Midwest Augustinian Province of Our Mother of Good Counsel)

that the "clericalization of women" would not solve existing problems and might even create new ones.

The Church has a different nature from social or political structures, he said, while recognizing and supporting the expansion of women's roles of governance and responsibility in various areas of ecclesial life, as seen with the appointment of women to prominent positions in the Roman Curia.

In the last interview Cardinal Prevost gave to *Vatican News* before becoming pope, he strongly reaffirmed the need to continue the

Pope Francis greets newly elevated Cardinal Robert F. Prevost during the consistory in St. Peter's Square at the Vatican Sept. 30, 2023. (CNS photo/Vatican Media, © Vatican Media)

reforms undertaken by Francis during his pontificate. "There is still much to be done, we must move forward. It is a spirit, a fundamental attitude for all of us," Prevost said:

> We cannot stop, we cannot turn back. We must see how the Holy Spirit wants the Church to be today and tomorrow, because the world in which the Church lives today is not the same as it was ten or twenty years ago. Therefore, the message is always the same: to proclaim Jesus Christ, to proclaim the Gospel. But the way to reach people today, young people, the

poor, politicians, is different.[14]

The Prophecy of Unity

Robert Francis Prevost's biography shows why his election to the papacy surprised all Vatican experts with its extraordinary speed.

The new pope has already defined his challenge to the world with the name he has chosen: Leo XIV. In his address to the cardinals on May 10, 2025, he revealed that there are several reasons for this decision, but the main one is this:

> Pope Leo XIII, with his historic encyclical *Rerum Novarum*, addressed the social question in the context of the first great industrial revolution; and today the Church offers to all its heritage of social doctrine to respond to another industrial revolution and the advances of artificial intelligence, which pose new challenges for the defense of human dignity, justice, and work.

To face this immense challenge, the Church needs unity, creativity, and dynamism. Now it has at its helm a humble man, in love with God, with an ardent missionary spirit. This man, an expert in building bridges, has performed the "miracle of unity" the conclave sought: He brings together in his person the hopes of cardinals of different sensibilities and tendencies. Now it is his turn to perform the miracle of unity in the Church so that it may enlighten and inspire the world of today.

Chapter 3

A New Pope for a New World

Twelve years have passed between the election of Pope Francis on March 12, 2013, and that of Pope Leo XIV. These years have nevertheless deepened the changes and challenges that humanity is going through.

Probably the most obvious shift is demographic and geopolitical, two deeply related dimensions. Our ingrained mental categories inherited the situation of the twentieth century, at the beginning of which countries with a Christian tradition carried decisive weight.

At the beginning of the twentieth century, the world population was 1.6 billion people: about 400 million Europeans (25 percent); between 80 and 160 million from the Americas (between 5 percent and 10 percent), two worlds considered as a Christian bloc. On the other side we had the "non-Christian" continents, such as Africa (8 percent, about 128 million people), Asia (more than 50 percent, exceeding 800 million people), and Oceania (less than 1 percent, about 6 to 10 million people).

Asia, the Great Challenge

The world of the twenty-first century has changed profoundly, with now more than 8 billion inhabitants. India, the country that has surpassed China in population, is moving toward 1.5 billion, almost as many as the entire human race at the beginning of the twentieth century.

This population growth also has a clear impact on economic and social development: India is on track to become the world's third-largest economy by 2027, surpassing Japan and Germany, according to Morgan Stanley's study "India's Impending Economic Boom" (November 8, 2022).

For Pope Leo XIV, this is a huge challenge, since only 2.3 percent of the inhabitants of India are Christians (data from The World Factbook) and, according to the latest version of the *Statistical Yearbook of the Church* (2023), only 1.7 percent are Catholics. The pontificate of Leo XIV will have to answer a difficult question: How is it possible that the beauty of the Christian Faith could not be shared in this great country which, according to tradition, received its first evangelization in the first century, through the work of the apostle Saint Thomas himself?

This small percentage of Catholics in India, totaling 23.4 million baptized individuals according to the latest edition of the *Statistical Yearbook of the Church*, should not be underestimated. India is today a real power in the world of Catholicism. It is the country with the largest number of seminarians preparing for the priesthood (11,401), followed by Brazil with 7,453 seminarians. India is one of the countries with the largest number of priests in absolute terms (34,079), which means that it has many more priests than the two countries with the largest number of Catholics in the world (Brazil, 23,184, and Mexico, 17,275). The number of Indian priests is approaching that of the United States (36,057).

India is the world's leading country in terms of the number of Catholic nuns — almost 100,000, much more than the United States (35,917) or Italy (63,721). Mathematically, we can say that most of the faces of priests and nuns in the future will have Indian features.

The other Asian giant, China, raises profound questions for Pope Leo. Some sources, such as the Center for Economics and Business Research's (CEBR) World Economic League Table 2023, predict that China's economy will overtake that of the United States by 2036.

According to The World Factbook, 5.1 percent of the population in China is Christian (among which 25 percent are estimated to be Catholic). For the safety of underground Catholic communities, the Vatican does not disclose official data on the exact number of Catholics in China.

As China's economic influence grows, so does its cultural influence in the world. This fact implies important questions for Pope Leo: Will Catholicism be able to challenge the Chinese heart to the point of proposing the Gospel as a horizon of life and happiness?

Chinese authorities are currently implementing a "Sinicization of religion" process launched by President Xi Jinping in 2016, which requires religious leaders and institutions to demonstrably embrace state socialism and the leadership of the Communist Party of China (CPC). Since 2018, new regulations on religious activities have been in effect in China, restricting religious practice and increasing state control over religious activities. Control over Catholic communities is exercised through the Catholic Patriotic Association (CPA), an organization founded in 1957 with the support of the People's Republic of China's Bureau of Religious Affairs.

The CPA is a major source of internal division among Catholics and tension with the Vatican, especially because it has historically claimed the right to elect and consecrate bishops without papal approval. This situation has led to the existence of two Catholic communities in China: an "official" one affiliated with the CPA, and an "underground" one that maintains loyalty to the pope and often operates in secret due to government restrictions.

Pope Francis sought to overcome these divisions at their root. An important milestone was the interim agreement signed in 2018 between the Holy See and the Chinese government on the appointment of bishops, a step toward reconciliation and regularization of the situation of bishops appointed without papal mandate. The Vatican and China renewed their agreement on October 22, 2024, extending its validity for another four years.

However, this agreement has also been the subject of criticism and concern within certain sectors of the Church, who see it as an excessive concession to Chinese government control. For their part, the authorities continue to restrict religious freedom in the country. Restrictions on religious practice, arrests of bishops or priests, and closures of unregistered churches continue to be reported.

The evangelization of China has been a historical challenge for the Church for two thousand years, since Catholicism has never been able to present itself as a way of life capable of attracting the majority of the population. Analysts believe that in the past, the Church has made the mistake of trying to impose Western categories, cultural customs, and language that are not essential to the Gospel. Today, evangelization is made even more difficult by the growing materialism and atheism in the country.

But the problem is also an opportunity. The question arises: How can the Catholic Church respond to the thirst for eternity of the Chinese heart, to which the regime proposes only a simple, practical materialism? The answer to this question will determine evangelization in the coming decades and the impact of the pontificate of Pope Leo XIV on a global scale.

The challenge can be extended more generally to Asia, where 60 percent of the world's population lives — about 4.6 billion people, for many of whom Jesus Christ is a great unknown. The presence of Catholics in Asian countries is statistically very marginal, except for East Timor (97 percent), the Philippines (83 percent), South Korea (11 percent), Hong Kong (8 percent), and Vietnam (7 percent).

What is certain is that, like never before, Rome will have to pay attention to what is happening in Asia.

United States, Hegemony Is Still in Place

While there are many predictions about when China and even India will overtake the United States economically, the answer is not clearcut. While China has made significant economic strides in recent years, current analyses suggest that its path to surpassing the United States as the world's largest economy is fraught with challenges. Revised projections and emerging economic headwinds indicate that this milestone may be delayed or may never materialize in the foreseeable future. The primary factor that could hinder China from overtaking the United States economically is its demographics: an aging population, low birth rates, and a shrinking workforce.

The world leadership of the United States and its influence on the rest of the planet have made the popes, especially since the Second World War, understand the importance of establishing constructive relations between the United States and the Church, which materialized with the opening of diplomatic relations on January 10, 1984, under the leadership of Ronald Reagan and John Paul II.

The understanding between the pope and much of the Catholic world in the United States (the fourth-largest Catholic country by number of baptized: 75.4 million, 22.5 percent of its population) has suffered moments of crisis during the pontificate of Francis.

The election of an American pope will have decisive consequences — and, in a way, consequences that were completely unforeseen until now. Pope Leo now faces the task of establishing a relationship with the U.S. administration, led by President Donald Trump. In this context, Prevost's election as pope introduces a new element of expectation. Despite his differences with Pope Francis, Trump made a point of traveling to Rome to attend the late pontiff's funeral. He has openly emphasized the importance of the Catholic vote, and for that reason, he is keen on maintaining a constructive institutional relationship with the new pope and the Church.

During Pope Francis's pontificate, tensions with the United States centered on Trump's immigration policies, including mass deportations, which the pope criticized for harming "the dignity of many men and women, and of entire families, and placing them in a state of particular vulnerability and defenselessness."[15]

The relationship between Rome and Washington is extremely important for the rest of the world. It has not only a political impact, but also a cultural one. Today, the United States plays a decisive role in shaping values through the media, music, cinema, video games, and other areas. The United States is not only the world's leading economic power, but also its leading cultural power. For the first time in history, the Church has an American pope — a pope capable of understanding the American mind-set, its values, and its potential. At the same time, he is a missionary who has spent much of his life outside of the United States. He is, therefore, a man with an exceptional capacity for objectivity. A new era is beginning in the relationship between the papacy and America.

Africa, Hope for Christianity?

Africa is home to about 16 percent of the world's population (1.35 billion people). The continent is in the midst of a period of demographic and economic growth.

In the last century, Africa has become the great hope of growth for Christianity in general and for the Catholic Church in particular. At the beginning of the twentieth century, there were only 1.9 million Catholics in Africa. Today, that number has grown dramatically, with 280.7 million Africans baptized in the Catholic Church, according to the latest data published by the *Statistical Yearbook of the Church*. Currently, one in five Catholics in the world is African. And given growth rates, Africa is expected to become the continent with the largest number of Catholics in the coming decades.

The increase in the number of African priests is already benefiting countries in Europe and the United States, which are welcoming young pastors to face the vocation crisis. Pope Leo XIV will have to find spaces where the pastors and faithful of the Catholic Church in Africa can express their spiritual richness in the service of the universal Church. The most eloquent gesture will be the further increase of the representation of Africans in the College of Cardinals as well as in the leadership of Vatican dicasteries.

The African Church might also have to focus on the challenges some members of the clergy are facing in the continent as to the respect of the promises of Catholic priests. In various African societies, celibacy is viewed as incompatible with cultural norms that emphasize procreation and family life. This cultural perspective can lead to difficulties for priests who are expected to remain celibate, as it may conflict with societal expectations and personal desires. As a result, some priests struggle to adhere to the vow of celibacy, leading to tensions between their sacramental promise and cultural context.

The pontificate of Pope Leo will need to pursue, among other important goals, a deep spiritual renewal among African bishops, priests, and seminarians — encouraging them to place the Gospel at the heart of their lives, choices, and witness above all other interests, including social recognition or material gain.

Two Contrasting Trends in the Arab World

The Arab world presents a particular challenge for Pope Leo XIV. While the rise of religious extremism has significantly complicated the lives of many Christians, the historically vibrant Catholic minority now finds itself largely dispersed in the diaspora. Some of these countries are in the process of losing their Christians. This is the case of Egypt (10 percent of the population is Christian), Syria (10 percent), Iraq (1 percent), Morocco (less than 1 percent), and Algeria (less than 1 percent).

The persecution and exodus of Christians from these Arab countries has been countered by another phenomenon that has not yet been much analyzed by experts: the integration of immigrant Catholics in Arab countries whose economies are flourishing because of oil. This is the case of Saudi Arabia (with 5.8 percent of baptized Catholics among its population), Qatar (11.5 percent), United Arab Emirates (8.2 percent), Kuwait (7.9 percent), and Bahrain (10.6 percent).

The pontificate of Pope Leo will be called on the one hand to show its particular consolation to the persecuted Christians in some of these Muslim-majority countries. The new pope is called to become the voice that Catholics do not have in Muslim-majority countries where there is still religious persecution. On the other hand, it will have to prove to their political leaders that the contribution of Christians to their society is a positive factor.

"Elder Brothers"

The war declared by Israel in October 2023, following the brutal Hamas attacks that left approximately 1,200 people dead, has not only caused tensions within the international community, but also between Jewish representatives and the Holy See. Amid a conflict that has left over 50,000 Palestinians dead,[16] it has been very difficult, even for Pope Francis, to find words that may transcend and penetrate the entrenched rhetoric of the conflicting parties.

Pope Leo is challenged to explore the theological and biblical relationships that underlie the dialogue between the "elder brothers" — as Pope John Paul II called the Jews — and Christians, an exercise promoted by the Latin Patriarch of Jerusalem, Cardinal Pierbattista Pizzaballa.

This deepening, called to alleviate the wounds of the past arising from the persecution of Jews at the hands of Christians, will allow relations between believers not to depend on the vagaries of politics, but to be based on something much deeper: the role played in the history of salvation by the people of the First Covenant, the unique and special relationship established between God and the Jewish people, as narrated in the Old Testament.

Europe

Even though nearly 40 percent of Europeans are Catholic, they have experienced a relative decline in their influence in the worldwide Church due to factors such as population growth (dramatically slowed in Europe) and the rise of the Church in other regions, particularly in Africa, Asia, and Latin America. This trend reflects changes in global Catholic demographics and is manifested in the diversification of Church leadership and in pastoral and theological priorities that reflect a wider range of cultural and social contexts.

In France, 74.9 percent of the population is baptized in the Catholic Church. According to an opinion poll conducted for the Catholic newspaper *La Croix* in 2017, 5 percent of the French population regularly goes to Mass, while 53 percent call themselves Catholic.

In Italy, where 97.1 percent of the population is baptized Catholic, 21 percent of people attended a place of worship once a week in 2020 (36 percent in 2001). In Spain, 93.3 percent of the population is baptized Catholic, and according to official data from the Center for Sociological Research (CIS) in February 2024, 17.9 percent considered themselves practicing Catholics.

In Germany, where 28.9 percent are baptized Catholics, the Church is experiencing an acute crisis. In 2024, 321,611 people formally left the Catholic Church in Germany, according to the German Bishops' Conference. While this figure is lower than the record 522,821 departures in 2022, it still represents a significant loss. The high number of departures has been attributed to several factors, including the church tax system, abuse scandals, and ideological divisions within the Church. In Germany, registered church members are required to pay an additional tax, prompting some to formally leave the Church to avoid this financial burden. The Evangelical Church in Germany (EKD) also experienced notable losses, with approximately 345,000 members leaving in 2024.

In Poland, 97.6 percent are baptized Catholics. According to data from the CBOS institute in December 2021, during the previous three decades the percentage of young people who regularly attended Catholic churches has dropped from 69 percent to 23 percent, and the number of nonpracticing Catholics has risen from 8 percent to 40 percent.

A worrying symptom is the demographic decline in Europe, which is particularly pronounced in Catholic countries such as Poland, Italy, and Spain. In 2023, Poland's population decreased by approximately 130,000 people, marking the largest decline among EU member states. The country has experienced a continuous decline in birth rates for fifteen consecutive years, reaching a record low of 379,000 births in 2023. Projections indicate that Italy's working-age population could decrease by nearly 19 percent by 2040, the most significant decline in Europe. In 2023, Spain registered 320,656 births, a 24 percent decrease compared to a decade earlier and the lowest number since 1941, just two years after the end of the Spanish Civil War.

In this new European context, the pontificate of Pope Leo XIV will, on the one hand, seal the loss of European representation in the universal Church, continuing the decline in the representativeness of cardinals from this continent, as well as of European collaborators in the Roman Curia. On the other hand, it will have to inspire and support the minorities of Catholics that make up the Church in the old continent, helping them to move from "passive majorities" to "creative minorities."

Russian Ice

The geopolitics of Pope Leo will also have to deal with the ice that the war in Ukraine has created in relations between Rome and Moscow. These relations have affected not only the pope's contacts with Vladimir Putin and his government, but also and above all with the Orthodox Church, since the Patriarch of Moscow, Kirill, has openly supported the conquest and annexation of Ukrainian territories. In Russia, a country with a Christian Orthodox majority, only 0.3 percent of the population is baptized Catholic.

The drama of the war has had terrible consequences for the Christian denominations in Ukraine. The majority of the population belongs to Orthodox parishes, which today are mainly divided between loyalty to the Moscow Patriarchate or the autocephalous (independent) Ukrainian Orthodox Church. Catholics make up 11.5 percent of the baptized.

With the wounds caused by the war still bleeding, Pope Leo's room for maneuver in his relations with Moscow will be very limited. After the military intervention, it will take many years, perhaps generations, for relations between Orthodox and Catholics in the region to return to an ecumenical spirit. But it is precisely in these situations that the Gospel message of Jesus Christ ("I tell you, love your enemies and pray for those who persecute you," Mt 5:44) is most fruitful.

Latin America, the New Missionary Continent

Pope St. John Paul II referred to Latin America as the "continent of hope," underscoring the region's immense spiritual, cultural, and social potential — home to 41.3 percent of the world's baptized Catholics.

Among the ten countries in the world with the highest number of Catholics, four are in Latin America: Brazil, Mexico, Colombia, and Argentina.

But the hope that the Polish pope saw in Latin America is in crisis for two reasons. First, because Latin American countries are experiencing a cascading process of secularization that extends the cultural models promoted by the United States and Europe. The effect of this phenomenon is a constant decrease in the religious practice of the baptized, with rates of religious practice that gradually tend to converge with those of the rest of the West.

Second, the lack of priests and resources present in rural or suburban areas has allowed evangelical and Pentecostal churches to spread throughout the continent. The lack of vocations to the priesthood in the Catholic Church implies a lack of ecclesial attention. In response, people seek to quench their spiritual thirst in other Christian groups, some of which are true cults. Political corruption, unemployment, economic crisis, and environmental degradation lead many believers to find in these groups a community that they cannot find in their poor Catholic parish.

Until a few years ago, the Catholic communities of Latin America were largely dependent on the contribution of missionary priests from Europe and the United States. The pontificate of Pope Leo XIV has the great challenge of transforming the Church in Latin America from a territory of missionaries to a protagonist of mission, not only in its own dioceses, but also in offering its human resources to other continents. In short, it is a matter of putting on the Christian world map the weight that the Church in Latin America has in numbers.

A New World for Pope Leo XIV

In the coming years, however, this whole scenario will be decisively altered by one crucial factor: fertility, which is insufficient today to maintain population levels in most countries.

An article on a large study published on May 18, 2024, by the scientific journal *The Lancet* warns of imbalances that are likely to become increasingly marked from one region of the world to another.[17] The study notes that more than half of the countries already have fertility rates that are too low to sustain their population levels. It adds that fertility rates will continue to decline worldwide in the future.

The researchers estimate that by 2050, 155 of 204 countries and territories (76 percent) will be below the replacement level of fertility. In developed countries, replacement level fertility can be taken as requiring an average of 2.1 children per woman.

The number of countries and territories below replacement level is predicted to further increase to 198 of 204 (97 percent) by 2100. This means that in these countries, populations will shrink unless low fertility can be offset by ethical and effective immigration. The extent of low fertility may also be mitigated in part by policies that offer greater support for the family. "These future trends in fertility rates and live births will completely reconfigure the global economy and the international balance of power and will necessitate reorganizing societies," the study explains.

Leo XIV will be the pope of a world with fewer and fewer children — a colossal challenge for the Catholic Church, which has historically found the family to be its natural environment for transmitting the Faith.

Chapter 4

A Pope for the End of Christendom

---✣---

Cardinal Robert Francis Prevost has been elected pope for a world that is witnessing the end of Christendom. The difference between Christendom and Christianity often generates confusion, but it is important to understand the difference to better understand the time the Church is going through.

At its core, Christianity is a religion rooted in love, faith, and a deep relationship with God, based on the teachings of Jesus Christ, whom Christians recognize as the Son of God and the Savior of mankind. The life, teachings, crucifixion, and resurrection of Jesus are fundamental to the Christian faith. As the world's most widely practiced religion, Christianity has billions of adherents in various denominations, including Catholicism, Protestantism, Anglicanism, Orthodoxy, and others.

Christendom, meanwhile, refers to the cultural, political, and social influence of Christianity as a dominant force, especially in areas where it shaped laws, culture, and governance. Christendom emphasized a unified identity among diverse peoples and nations under the banner of the Christian faith, despite the reality of differing interpretations, practices, and political ambitions among them.

Historians believe that Christendom began when Christianity became the official religion of the Roman Empire in A.D. 380 through the Edict of Thessalonica, promulgated by Emperor Theodosius I, who sought to unify the empire under the Christian faith. Although two thousand years have passed since the death and resurrection of Jesus, it can be said that the adventure of Christianity has just begun, and its future is still full of surprises. However, Christendom has become an obsolete phenomenon.

Christendom, a Way of Thinking

As explained in *From Christendom to Apostolic Mission: Pastoral Strategies for an Apostolic Age* (University of Mary, 2020), when the Christian narrative of the human drama and its corresponding moral order have become prominent in a given society and have come to provide, at least largely, that society's ruling vision, what emerges can be called a "Christendom culture."

A Christendom culture not only influences the organization of society but moves forward under the imaginative vision and narrative provided by Christianity, regardless of the specific politics of its establishment.

In the societies forged by Christendom, the majority of the members were not necessarily Christians seriously committed to their faith. There was a general acceptance of basic Christian truths and an adoption of the Christian narrative and vision of the world around which the institutions of society were organized. To call such a society Christian does not mean that the majority of its members were serious or educated Christians; in fact, there has probably never been a human society in which that was the case.

The Apostolic Era
The testimony of faith that Christians gave before their religion became the official religion of the Roman Empire happened in a historical context that is unrepeatable today. The Christians of the first generations, and with them the world, discovered the religion of love from the lips of witnesses to the preaching of the apostles. The proclamation of Jesus of Nazareth, God made man to save humanity, became a disruptive message in the face of the dominant cruelty of the Roman Empire.

These were years in which, for Christians, everything was yet to be discovered. Despite internal disputes due to doctrinal divergences, Christians were spreading throughout the Roman Empire with surprising contagiousness. The persecutions that the emperors soon unleashed against the followers of Jesus did not stop them. On the contrary, the blood of the martyrs became the seed of new Christians, as Tertullian wrote in the year 197. The same author, himself a Christian convert, also wrote the famous phrase that the pagans uttered when they saw the martyrdom of the Christians: "See how they love one another. See how they are willing to die for each other."

From Christendom to Apostolic Mission distinguishes between the "apostolic era" of Christianity (the first four centuries), because of its temporal proximity to the evangelizing work of the first apostles, and "Christendom," which characterizes the subsequent history of Christianity.

Post-Christendom, Not Post-Christianity
The same book considers that Christianity has the challenge to live a new apostolic era like the first Christians. However, at the time of the first disciples of Jesus, Christianity appeared as something completely new. Today, people consider that they already know what Christianity has to offer.

British author C. S. Lewis explained the difference between the two models with a striking example: A man courting a young maiden is not the same as a man courting a cynical divorcée to return to her former marriage. The situation is even more complex when we consider that many who have abandoned Christianity and embraced an entirely different worldview still call themselves Christians.

Other observers call the present phase the "post-Christian era." This is a terminological error, for Christianity is still very much alive in the hearts, lives, and communities of millions and millions of people in its various denominations and across continents. Numerically, there have never been so many convinced Christian believers on the face of the earth as there are now.

More precise is the term *postmodernity*, created to describe the cultural and intellectual climate that emerged in the latter half of the twentieth century, characterized by a rejection of the grand narratives and certainties of modernity.

Postmodernity is characterized by an attitude of skepticism toward general narratives that attempt to explain broad aspects of human experience and history, especially religion. This leads to a relativistic perspective that values diversity of opinion and questions the existence of universal truths, privileging individual or cultural interpretations of reality. It emphasizes the importance of cultural, ethnic, sexual, and gender diversity, rejecting binary classifications and encouraging the recognition and appreciation of multiple identities and perspectives.

Now, if we want to analyze this period from a more strictly religious point of view, we can conclude that Pope Leo XIV is facing an era of post-Christendom — that is, an era in which Christianity has lost its dominant social and institutional role, but in which Christians are still dynamic, although they have become minorities.

Creative Minorities

In this context, Pope Benedict XVI borrowed the term *creative minorities* from the British historian Arnold Toynbee (1889–1975). The historian explained that civilizations collapse primarily because of internal decline rather than external attack. "Civilizations," Toynbee wrote, "die by suicide, not by murder."

The creative minorities, Toynbee argued, are those who proactively respond to a civilizational crisis and whose response allows that civilization to grow. An example was the response of the Catholic Church to the collapse of the Roman Empire in the West in the fifth century. The Church responded by preserving the wisdom and law of Athens, Rome, and Jerusalem, while integrating the invading Gothic tribes into a universal religious community. Western civilization was thus saved and enriched.

The creative minorities in the post-Christendom era recognize, first, that being an active Christian is now a choice rather than a matter of social conformity. This means that Christians of the future will be active believers because they have chosen to live out the teachings of Jesus.

"An Epochal Change"

"We are not living an epoch of change so much as an epochal change." This phrase, spoken by Cardinal Jorge Mario Bergoglio, was decisive for his appointment as pope in the conclave convened after the resignation of Benedict XVI.

Humanity is undergoing a truly epochal change after the end of Christendom. There are moments in human history when waves of change sweep through societies, reshaping their very identity. These moments mark not just an era of ephemeral change, but a profound transition from one epoch to another. In our day, it is becoming increasingly clear that we are not simply witnessing an era of change, but we are experiencing a transformative change: "an epochal change."

This was one of the central elements of the final message of the Fifth Episcopal Conference of Latin America and the Caribbean (known as the Aparecida Conference).[18] The principal author of the closing message was Cardinal Jorge Mario Bergoglio, then the archbishop of Buenos Aires. His message invited the Church to move beyond peripheral issues and address the fundamental challenges that humanity faces today.

The explosion of communications, the globalization of the economy, the development of technology and science, the massive phenomenon of migration, the mixing of cultures, and the religious pluralism of our societies have created a new world — not because of geographical expansion, but because of the complexity of social relations resulting from so many changes, the pace of which we can hardly follow and the meaning of which we can hardly understand.

This epochal shift has a surprising accelerating factor: the unprecedented technological revolution that is affecting all dimensions of human existence. Just think of the impact on humanity of the advent of artificial intelligence and the way it is transforming not only production processes and working conditions, but even human creativity and imagination itself.

The internet has not only changed the way we live and work, it also has a transformative impact on human relationships. Think of the disruptive influence of social networks on education and even on people's deeply personal lives. Consider, for instance, that the internet has become the first place people look for a romantic partner.

We are only at the beginning of the impact that new technologies will have on medicine, including genetic engineering, which, if uncontrolled, could lead to scenarios with unknown consequences.

New technologies have resurrected ancient myths sought and pursued by transhumanist currents, according to which the use of advanced technology and other forms of human intervention will be able to enhance human physical and cognitive capabilities to the point of achieving significantly longer lives and even, for some obsessed individuals, the goal of immortality.

In fact, as Cardinal Marc Ouellet, prefect emeritus of the Vatican Dicastery for Bishops, explained in the German edition of the magazine *Communio*, the epochal change is perhaps most evident in anthropology.[19]

"Human identity has become a field of experimentation," explains the Canadian cardinal. "It is the subject of the ideologization of decisions and relationships. This poses huge challenges for families, schools and society, as well as for the transmission of cultural heritage. For we are not dealing with a temporary crisis here, we are not living in a time of confusing transition to a new humanism. Rather, this new situation must be accepted as permanent. The traditional rational points of reference can no longer claim exclusivity. In short, the epochal change includes pluralism as a constitutive element of every society in a globalized world."

We can no longer dream of returning to a previous state of affairs once the current crisis has been calmed and overcome. "In other words, we need to think about the future of Christianity in a context that expects Christians to find a new paradigm for witnessing to their identity," Ouellet underlines. He then concludes, "We must therefore look to cultural and religious diversity with a spirit of dialogue, offering the Christian vision in all gratuitousness and with concern for human fraternity."

The Crisis of Meaning

In fact, what characterizes the men and women who surf these changing times is precisely the lack of meaning: the element capable of offering social cohesion, beyond the increasingly fragmented ideological and political categories. This crisis of meaning is what unites more and more people because of the uncertainty caused by the profound changes the world is undergoing.

Let's take an example that may be revealing: gender identity. For some highly influential ideologies today, it is considered a personal choice. Meanwhile, in its two thousand years of history, the Church has maintained that gender identity is intrinsically linked to biology and human nature, affirming that God created human beings as "male and female" (Gn 1:27). This issue presents enormous challenges in education for families and schools, as well as for the shared vision of a community and the transmission of cultural heritage.

The consequence of this crisis of meaning is secularization and the loss of transcendence. The growing religious indifference of Western societies has led to a distancing from God and religion, with a double effect.

First, it is becoming much more difficult for anyone to find the transcendent meaning of their lives. Postmodernity has brought with it a profound questioning of the meaning of human existence, identity, and the purpose of life, without offering definitive answers. Moreover, the prevailing mind-set insists that these questions do not exist, making any attempt to find an answer to them pointless.

Second, the crisis of meaning makes it more difficult for people to feel and experience that they are part of the same community with shared transcendent values. Humanity finds that it no longer has a shared worldview that would enable men and women to face emerging challenges from a renewed perspective. The lack of moral consensus and the "individualization" or "relativization" of values have made it difficult to build a solid ethical framework that provides a sense of direction and purpose.

Thus, on the one hand, an acute individualism has emerged, which explains above all the current family crisis. Suicide has become an epidemic among young people in the United States and Europe. In North America, the suicide rate among young people aged ten to twenty-four years increased by 52.2 percent between 2000 and 2021. Suicide became the second leading cause of death for this age group, according to the Centers for Disease Control and Prevention.[20]

The same is true in Europe, where suicide is also becoming the second leading cause of death among young people aged ten to nineteen, according to a UNICEF study published October 15, 2021. In some countries, such as Belgium, suicide is already the leading cause of death among young people aged fifteen to twenty-four (one in four deaths).

Loneliness is also one of today's social epidemics, so much so that some governments have developed ministries to address the issue — for example, the British government has created the Ministry of Loneliness. These government initiatives aim to combat loneliness and its effects on the population, which can be as detrimental to health as smoking fifteen cigarettes a day. Although this phenomenon affects all age groups, it is the elderly who are most affected. In England, it is estimated that half of all 75-year-olds live alone.

The famous statistic that half of all marriages in America end in divorce is confirmed by the Centers for Disease Control and Prevention.[21] This is true, but only for first marriages, half of which end in divorce. Second and third marriages fail at a much higher rate. The average length of marriage before divorce is eight years — a shorter period of time than an ordinary loan at the bank to buy a house.

In the midst of this lack of meaning, the degradation of the environment and the effects of climate change are causing existential panic among younger generations, to the point that young couples are questioning whether to have children so as not to be forced to live in a spoiled world and to avoid contributing to its polluting degradation. It is one of the factors that explains the worldwide decline in fertility to which we referred in the conclusion of Chapter 3.

The Great Opportunity for Pope Leo XIV

Every crisis is an opportunity. And the current crisis of meaning challenges Christians and, of course, the new pope to rise to this great opportunity.

After all, it is possible now more than ever for the richness of the Gospel of Jesus Christ to become a reason for hope for men and women in this post-Christian era. In this existential crisis, Christianity can become a reference of life for contemporary society for three obvious reasons.

- Primarily, because it offers a well-defined value system based on charity, compassion, forgiveness, and transcendence. These values can provide a sense of purpose and guidance amid postmodern individualism.
- Second, because the Christian faith presents a worldview that conceives of an order and a divine plan for the universe and human existence, which becomes a basis for hope in the face of the apparent meaninglessness and chaos experienced by postmodern men and women.
- Third, Jesus' teachings on the dignity of every human being, the importance of helping others, and the search for peace and justice are authentic sources of inspiration in the face of contemporary social challenges.

The Church and the Gospel of Jesus Christ in this epochal change have the authentic disruptive capacity to make human beings experience that they are children of God, members of a community of brothers and sisters, called to the same vocation: to find happiness.

By following in the footsteps of Leo XIII, the new pope demonstrates that he is fully aware of the epochal change in which we live. The great challenge of his pontificate as the pope of the end of Christendom becomes, in reality, the great historical opportunity of the Church. Will Jesus' followers be credible witnesses of his love? Perhaps the person who will have to answer this question with his life most clearly and publicly is Pope Leo XIV.

Chapter 5

The Numbers of the Catholic Church of Pope Leo XIV

---✢---

The situation of the Catholic Church at the beginning of the pontificate of Pope Leo may appear to be one of the most difficult in its two-thousand-year history. In general, analyses of the vitality of the Church depend too much on the ideological or affective position with which the analyst faces reality. To avoid this temptation, it is very useful to let the numbers speak for themselves.

Religious "Nones" Are the Largest Single Group in the United States

If the end of Christendom means the loss of the Church's dominant influence in society, then the latest figures from the United States are particularly eloquent.

A study from Pew Research, published on January 24, 2024, concludes that religious "nones" are now the largest single group in the United States.[22] When Americans are asked to check a box indicating their religious affiliation, 28 percent check "none." They are part of a group that includes atheists, agnostics, and those who say their religion is "nothing in particular." They're more prevalent among American adults than Catholics (23 percent) or evangelical Protestants (24 percent). In 2007, nones made up just 16 percent of Americans, but Pew's new survey of more than 3,300 U.S. adults shows that number has grown dramatically.

They are not all antireligious. Most nones say religion does some harm, but many also think it does some good. Most have a more positive view of science than the religiously affiliated, but they reject the idea that science can explain everything.

Attendance at weekly Mass among U.S. Catholics has declined to an average of just over 20 percent in 2023 and the first months of 2024, according to the study published on the blog of the Center for Applied Research in the Apostolate (CARA) at Georgetown University.[23] Certain celebrations in the liturgical calendar, such as Ash Wednesday or Easter, still attract more than 50 percent of Catholics.

These numbers are similar to those in European countries with a Catholic tradition, such as Italy. According to the Italian National Statistics Institute (ISTAT), in 2020 in this country, 21 percent of people over the age of six attended a place of worship at least once a week (36 percent in 2001), while 29 percent never attended a place of worship (16 percent in 2001).

Decrease in the Number of Baptisms

We present in this chapter an unpublished study, which is based on the comparison between the 2023 edition of the Statistical Yearbook of the Church (the latest available), published by the Vatican, and the 2000 edition. The analysis shows that worldwide there is a difference of five million fewer baptisms (-27.6 percent) between one year and the other.

Baptisms in the Catholic Church

■ Baptisms 2000 ■ Baptisms 2023

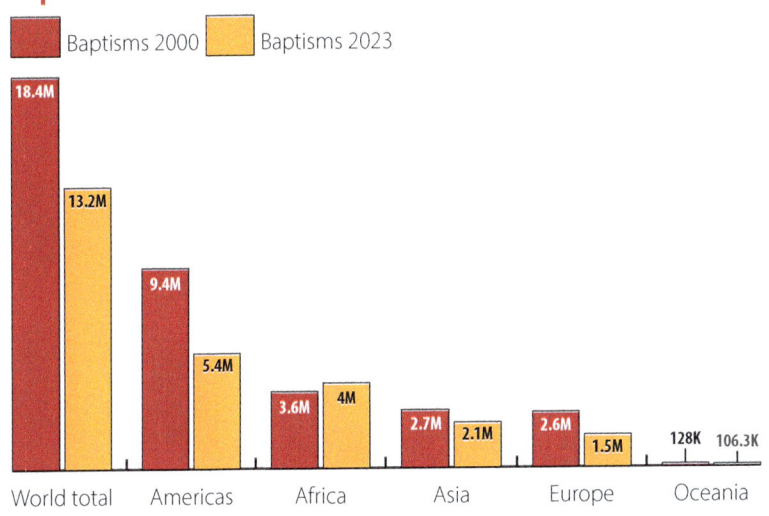

Region	2000	2023
World total	18.4M	13.2M
Americas	9.4M	5.4M
Africa	3.6M	4M
Asia	2.7M	2.1M
Europe	2.6M	1.5M
Oceania	128K	106.3K

Source: Statistical Yearbook of the Church 2000 and 2023

This worldwide negative trend is observed in all continents, with the sole exception of Africa, where 446,211 more baptisms were administered in 2023 than in 2000 (+11.1 percent). In the Americas, there is a reduction of 42.3 percent, in Europe 41.2 percent, in Asia it falls by 23.6 percent, and in Oceania the decline is 16.9 percent.

In the United States, the number of baptisms went from 1,097,290 in 2000 to 587,302 in 2023 (-53.5 percent). A similar decrease was experienced by Brazil, with 2,163,086 in 2000 and 1,128,824 in 2023 (-47.8 percent). The COVID pandemic did not have a decisive impact on the number of new baptisms, as the downward trend has been confirmed by previous years.

Yet, since the number of Catholics who die each year is less than the number who are baptized, the total number of Catholics in the world continues to grow. According to the Statistical Yearbook of the Church, there were more than 1.4 billion Catholics in the world in 2023, up from 1.0 billion in 2000. This is an increase of 34.5 percent. This means that 17.8 percent of the world's population is Catholic.

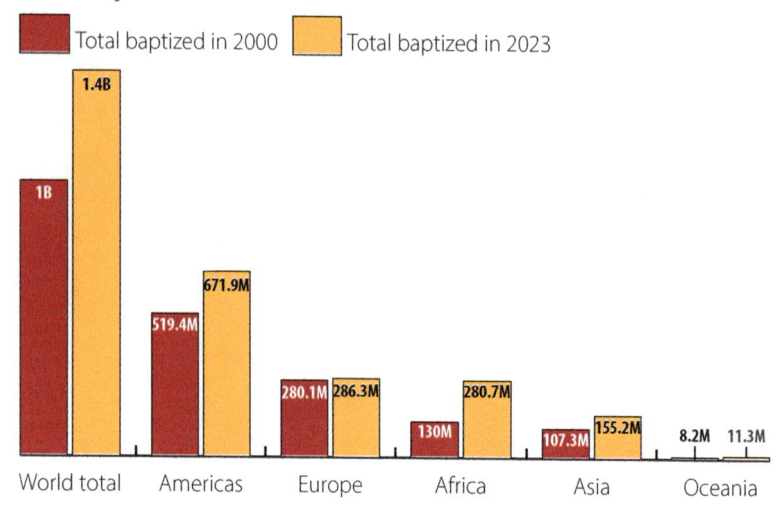

Total Baptized

Legend: Total baptized in 2000 | Total baptized in 2023

Region	2000	2023
World total	1B	1.4B
Americas	519.4M	671.9M
Europe	280.1M	286.3M
Africa	130M	280.7M
Asia	107.3M	155.2M
Oceania	8.2M	11.3M

Source: Statistical Yearbook of the Church 2000 and 2023

The country with the largest number of baptized in the Catholic Church is Brazil (182.1 million), an increase of 26.6 percent over 2000, followed by Mexico with 119.9 million (+33.7 percent in this period), the Philippines with 93.2 million (+47.9 percent), the United States with 75.4 million (+19.2 percent), Italy with 57.3 million (+2.6 percent), the Democratic Republic of the Congo with 54.8 million (+102.8 percent), France with 49.3 million (+5.4 percent), Colombia with 48.8 million (+29.6 percent), Spain with 44.8 million (+20.7 percent), and Argentina with 42.7 million (+27.6 percent).

The Deepest Crisis: Catholic Marriages

Along with baptisms and religious practice, marriages within the Church are another crucial index for understanding the vitality of Catholicism. From 3.7 million marriages in 2000, the number has fallen to 1.8 million, a decrease of 50.5 percent.

Marriages in the Catholic Church

- Marriages 2000
- Marriages 2023

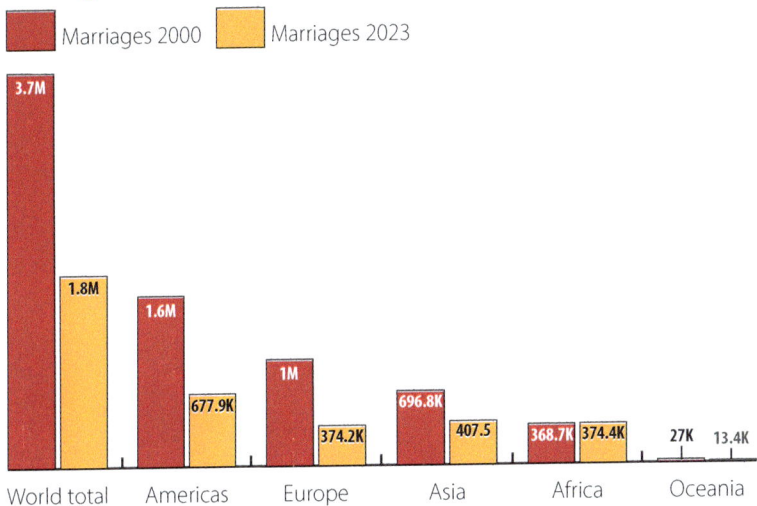

	World total	Americas	Europe	Asia	Africa	Oceania
2000	3.7M	1.6M	1M	696.8K	368.7K	27K
2023	1.8M	677.9K	374.2K	407.5	374.4K	13.4K

Source: Statistical Yearbook of the Church 2000 and 2023

In the United States, the number of Catholic marriages has dropped from 260,665 in 2000 to 109,027, a decrease of 58.2 percent. The situation is even more serious in other large Catholic countries. In Mexico, which today is the country with the highest number of marriages celebrated in the Church, it has gone from 396,019 marriages in 2000 to 178,399 in 2023 (-55 percent), and in Brazil from 368,672 to 186,485 (-49 percent).

In Europe, the trend is similar. In France, it has gone from 122,580 marriages in 2000 to 41,402 in 2021 (-66.3 percent); in Italy, from 248,920 to 88,109 (-64.6 percent); and in Ireland, from 17,866 to 9,402 (-47.4 percent). Spain breaks records with a free fall in marriages from 165,704 to 32,851 (-80.2 percent). In Nigeria, on the other hand, the number rose from 59,259 to 70,186, an increase of 18.4 percent.

Priests: Reality Is Not Always What It Seems

The decline in vocations to the priesthood in the West is often considered one of the greatest concerns for the future of the Catholic Church. However, unlike marriages, the numbers tell a different story.

Total Number of Priests

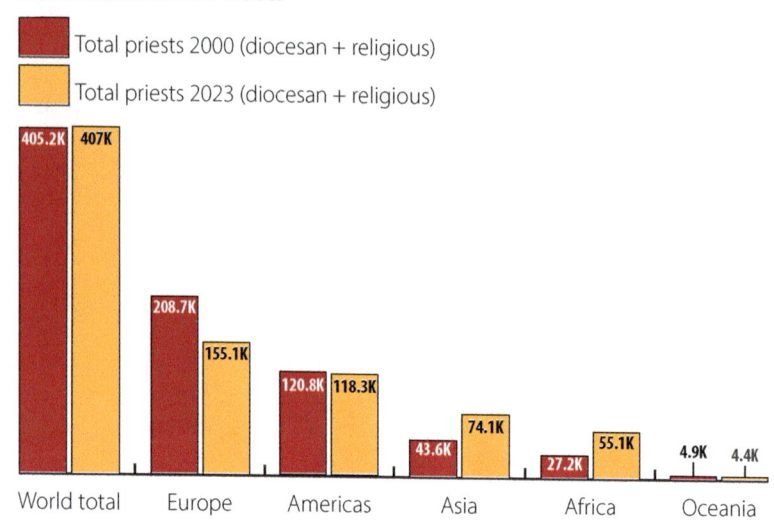

- Total priests 2000 (diocesan + religious)
- Total priests 2023 (diocesan + religious)

Region	2000	2023
World total	405.2K	407K
Europe	208.7K	155.1K
Americas	120.8K	118.3K
Asia	43.6K	74.1K
Africa	27.2K	55.1K
Oceania	4.9K	4.4K

Source: Statistical Yearbook of the Church 2000 and 2023

The number of priests in the world went from 405,200 in 2000 to 406,996 in 2023, an increase of 0.4 percent. Certainly, in Europe the decrease is clear: 25.7 percent. In the Americas and Oceania, however, the figures are almost unchanged. In Asia and Africa, the increase is very strong: +70 percent and +103 percent, respectively.

In the United States, the number of priests decreased from 48,288 to 36,057, a decrease of 25.3 percent. These figures do not include an important fact for understanding the situation on the ground: the increase in the average age of priests. Researchers at CARA found that the average age of Catholic priests in the United States has risen from 35 in 1970 to 63 in 2009. And the average age has continued to rise in recent years, although no official figures have been published.

In Europe, one of the countries where the decrease of priests is more intense is France, where it has gone from 25,353 priests in 2000 to 13,600 in 2021 — a decrease of 49.3 percent. According to the 2023 edition of the Statistical Yearbook of the Catholic Church in France, published by the French Bishops' Conference, the average

age of priests there is 72.2 years. This makes the French clergy one of the oldest in Europe.

In Spain, where the number of priests has decreased by 32.6 percent in the period analyzed (from 27,281 in 2000 to 18,391 priests in 2023), the average age is sixty-three years, according to journalistic sources consulted.

Ireland has lost 36.3 percent of its priests in these two decades (from 5,642 to 3,592). A survey conducted by the Association of Catholic Priests (ACP) in that country, published in November 2022, shows that almost 15 percent of priests are over seventy-five and still working, and more than 25 percent are between the ages of sixty and seventy-five.

Between 2000 and 2023, the number of priests decreased in Italy (-27 percent), Germany (-32.5 percent), and Great Britain (-27.4 percent). Poland has been an exception in Europe, with an increase of 5.5 percent in the number of priests during the period analyzed.

These figures contrast with those of the African countries. In Nigeria, the increase of priests has reached 186.7 percent (from 3,597 in 2000 to 10,309 in 2021) and in the Democratic Republic of Congo 67.9 percent (from 3,937 to 6,609).

In Brazil the number of priests increased by 39.7 percent (from 16,598 to 23,184), in Mexico by 23 percent (from 14,049 to 17,275), while in Argentina it decreased by 12 percent (from 5,868 to 5,160).

In the Philippines, the number of priests increased by 41.8 percent (from 7,500 to 10,662).

In India, where only 1.7 percent of the population is baptized in the Catholic Church, the increase in the number of priests remains impressive: During the period analyzed, they rose from 19,404 to 34,079, an increase of 75.6 percent.

Even though the number of priestly ordinations per year decreased by 16 percent between 2000 and 2023 (from 9,376 to 7,872), the total number of priests increased because the mortality rate among priests was lower than the number of priests ordained.

Ordination of Diocesan Priests

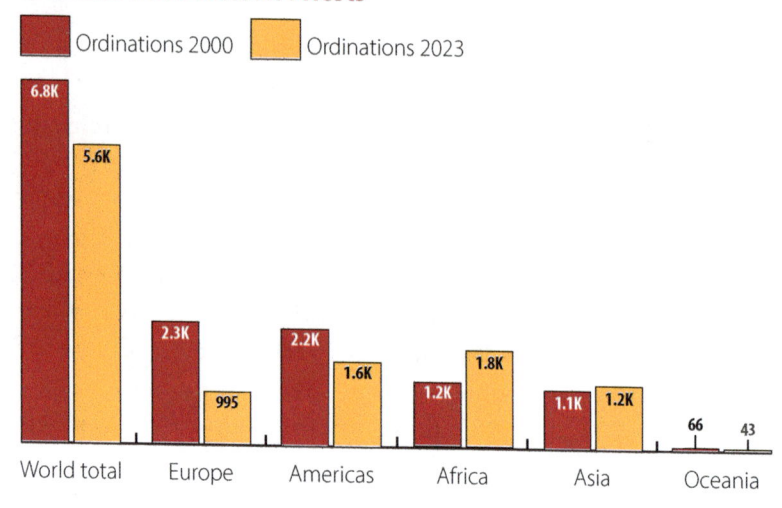

■ Ordinations 2000   ■ Ordinations 2023

Region	2000	2023
World total	6.8K	5.6K
Europe	2.3K	995
Americas	2.2K	1.6K
Africa	1.2K	1.8K
Asia	1.1K	1.2K
Oceania	66	43

Source: Statistical Yearbook of the Church 2000 and 2023

If we consider only the ordinations of diocesan priests (those who depend directly on the bishop of a diocese and not on a congregation or religious order), we see that there were 6,814 in the year 2000, compared to 5,621 in 2023 — a decrease of 17.51 percent.

This figure is closely linked to the number of seminarians, which worldwide experienced a reduction of 3.7 percent, from 110,583 in 2000 to 106,495 in 2023.

Number of Seminarians

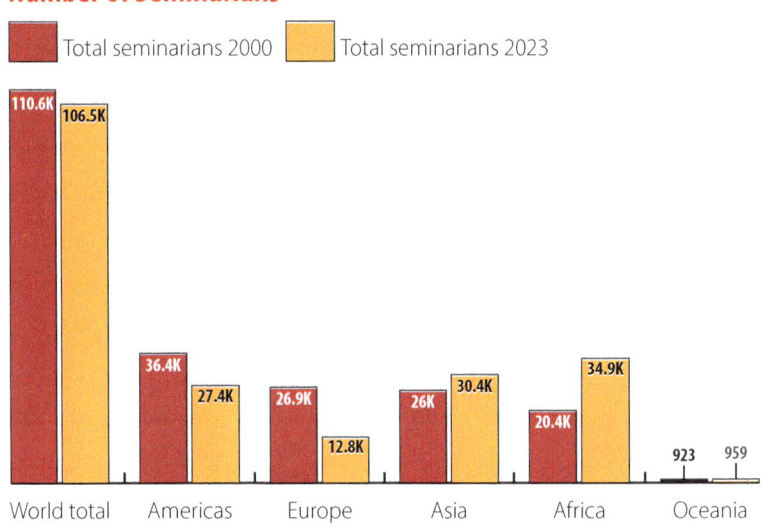

■ Total seminarians 2000   ■ Total seminarians 2023

Region	2000	2023
World total	110.6K	106.5K
Americas	36.4K	27.4K
Europe	26.9K	12.8K
Asia	26K	30.4K
Africa	20.4K	34.9K
Oceania	923	959

Source: Statistical Yearbook of the Church 2000 and 2023

As mentioned previously, India is the country with the highest number of seminarians in the world, with 11,401. It is followed by Brazil (7,453), the Philippines (6,473), Nigeria (6,333), Mexico (4,818), the United States (4,521), and both the Democratic Republic of the Congo and Italy, each with 4,155 candidates for the priesthood.

Seminarians vs. Diocesan Priests

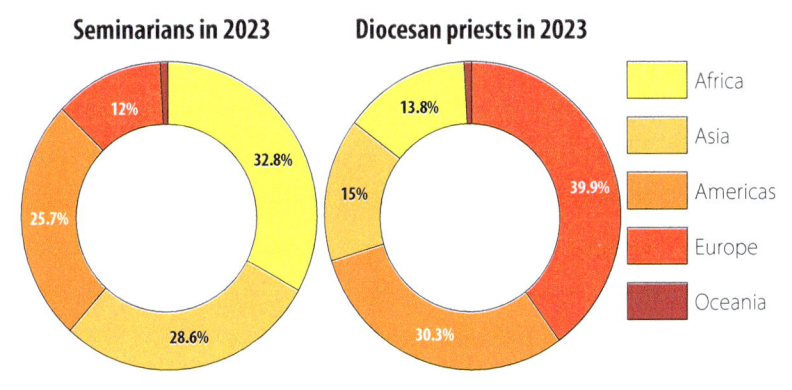

Seminarians in 2023
- Africa: 32.8%
- Asia: 28.6%
- Americas: 25.7%
- Europe: 12%

Diocesan priests in 2023
- Africa: 13.8%
- Asia: 15%
- Americas: 30.3%
- Europe: 39.9%

Source: Statistical Yearbook of the Church 2000 and 2023

The comparison between seminarians and diocesan priests offers an interesting picture of the future of the Church. Europe, once the cradle of priests (39.9 percent of priests), will become a minority (12 percent of seminarians), while the majority of seminarians today are in Africa (32.8 percent) and Asia (28.6 percent), which means that these two continents will one day have the majority of Catholic priests in the world.

Religious Women Are Also Decreasing

Once again, the numbers contradict appearances. The number of priests worldwide is increasing, albeit very slightly, while the number of women religious is decreasing sharply, by 26.4 percent worldwide (from 801,185 to 589,423). The number of religious sisters is increasing in Africa (61.6 percent) and Asia (27.1 percent), while the decline is significant in Europe (-49.3 percent), in the Americas (-41.1 percent), and in Oceania (-48.1 percent).

Number of Women Religious

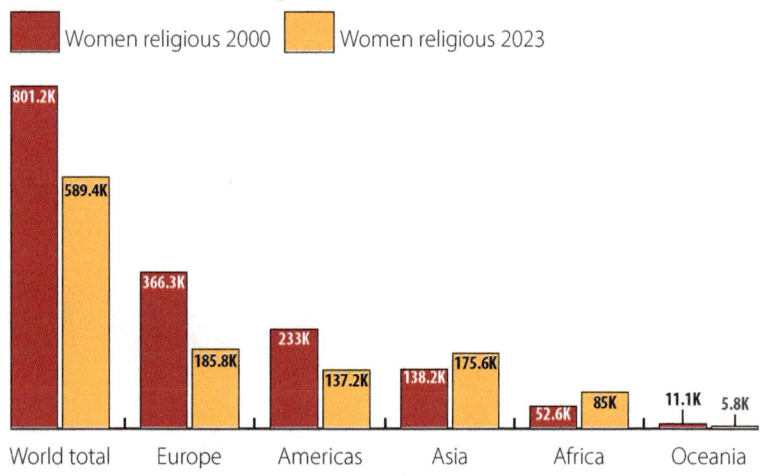

Region	Women religious 2000	Women religious 2023
World total	801.2K	589.4K
Europe	366.3K	185.8K
Americas	233K	137.2K
Asia	138.2K	175.6K
Africa	52.6K	85K
Oceania	11.1K	5.8K

Source: Statistical Yearbook of the Church 2000 and 2023

Once again, the strength of India, where 98,646 religious live today, is surprising, followed by Italy with 63,721, the United States with

35,917, Spain with 34,347, Mexico with 23,453, Brazil with 22,823, and France with 18,330.

The "Boom" of Lay Men and Women

An interesting element of the face of the Catholic Church in the third millennium is the constant increase in the number of laypeople who actively participate in the evangelizing work of the Church. This is one of the fruits of the Second Vatican Council (1962–65).

In less than a quarter of a century, the number of catechists worldwide increased by 8.52 percent, with the most significant growth seen in Asia (42.77 percent), Africa (21.04 percent), and the Americas (6.67 percent). The number remained stable in Oceania and declined in Europe (-10.50 percent).

Number of Catechists

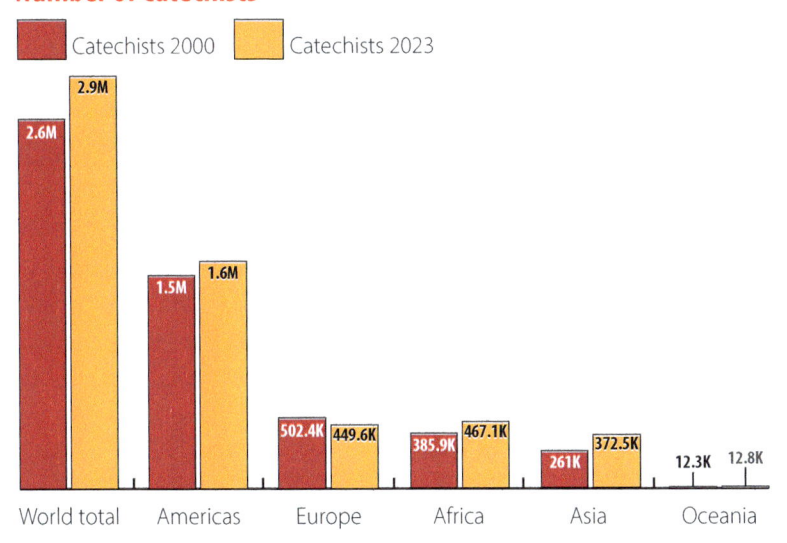

Region	Catechists 2000	Catechists 2023
World total	2.6M	2.9M
Americas	1.5M	1.6M
Europe	502.4K	449.6K
Africa	385.9K	467.1K
Asia	261K	372.5K
Oceania	12.3K	12.8K

Source: Statistical Yearbook of the Church 2000 and 2023

The giant in the number of catechists is Brazil with 469,172, followed by Mexico (278,548), United States (270,487), Italy (219,938), India (122,146), the Philippines (104,986), and Spain (81,675). The surprisingly low number of catechists in Poland (9,514) is a numerical manifestation of a Church in which the figure of the priest is still central to the life of parish communities.

But the great surprise in the Church's numbers in the middle of the third decade of the third millennium is the "boom" in lay missionaries. This figure, which is not yet clearly institutionalized in the dioceses, refers to laymen and women carrying out missionary work in parishes or Catholic communities and movements, either on a full-time or volunteer basis.

Lay missionaries can be involved in a wide range of missionary activities, such as evangelization, humanitarian service, social justice, community development, and interfaith dialogue. They contribute to the Church's mission of spreading the Good News and building a more just and compassionate society.

For the first time in history, the number of lay missionaries (444,606) has surpassed that of priests (406,996) in the Catholic Church.

This development aligns with the Second Vatican Council's call for greater lay involvement in the Church's apostolic activities, emphasizing the universal call to mission by bringing the Gospel to diverse communities worldwide.

Worldwide, the number of lay missionaries increased by 251.9 percent between 2000 and 2023. This is mainly a phenomenon in Latin American countries, which have been able to respond to the low ratio of priests per baptized. This is the case, for example, in Brazil with 121,408 lay missionaries (293 percent more than in 2000), in Colombia with 72,958 (236 percent), and in Mexico with 53,921 (an impressive growth of 2,006 percent).

Latin American countries with a much smaller number of baptized also have a high number of missionaries: Guatemala (38,667), Nicaragua (12,975), and Venezuela (19,757) have many more lay missionaries than countries with a large number of baptized, such as the United States (4,667), France (2,215), Italy (1,479), Germany (861), and Spain (98).

Number of Lay Missionaries

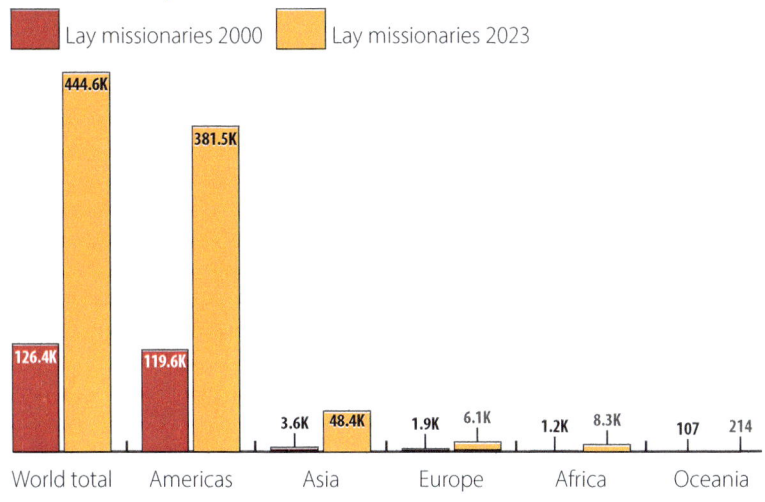

■ Lay missionaries 2000   ■ Lay missionaries 2023

	World total	Americas	Asia	Europe	Africa	Oceania
2000	126.4K	119.6K	3.6K	1.9K	1.2K	107
2023	444.6K	381.5K	48.4K	6.1K	8.3K	214

Source: Statistical Yearbook of the Church 2000 and 2023

A Planetary Educational Work

The Church has always given great importance to the work of education as an environment for the transmission of the Faith, the integral formation of the person, the promotion of social justice, and the encouragement of dialogue between faith and reason.

This work, which is also recognized by many believers of other denominations who enroll their children in these schools, continues to grow. Between 2000 and 2023, the number of students in Catholic schools increased by 41.3 percent (from 45.7 million to 64.5 million), thanks in particular to a 128.6 percent increase in the number of students in Africa. The increase remains significant in Asia (31.9 percent) and in Oceania (37.1 percent). Even in Europe, the number of students increased slightly (1.7 percent).

Students in Catholic Schools

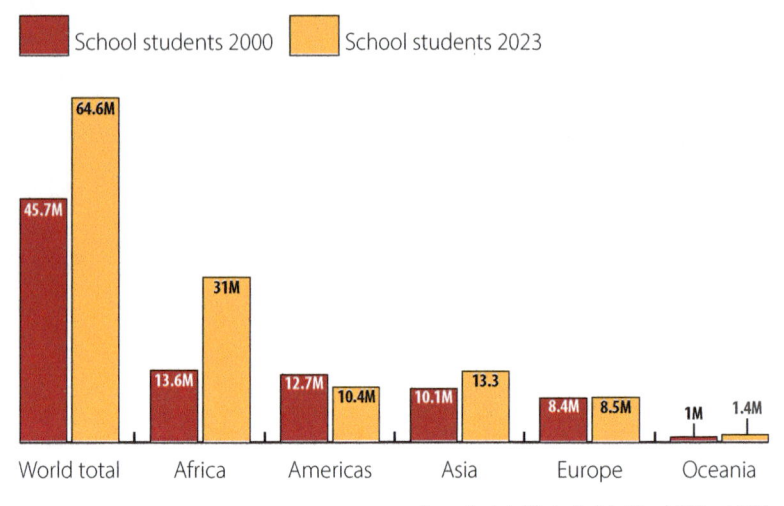

■ School students 2000   ■ School students 2023

Region	2000	2023
World total	45.7M	64.6M
Africa	13.6M	31M
Americas	12.7M	10.4M
Asia	10.1M	13.3M
Europe	8.4M	8.5M
Oceania	1M	1.4M

Source: Statistical Yearbook of the Church 2000 and 2023

In the United States, there is a clear trend in the opposite direction, as the number of students in Catholic schools has decreased significantly. It went from 2.6 million in 2000 to 1.7 million in 2023, a decrease of 34.6 percent. An analogous phenomenon can be observed in Brazil, where the number of students in these schools has decreased by 41.2 percent (from 1.5 million to 960,653), as well as in Mexico, although in this country the decrease is less marked (-7.2 percent, from 1,084,862 to 1,006,527).

The boom in Catholic schools is particularly strong in the Democratic Republic of Congo, where between 2000 and 2023 the number of students in Catholic schools increased by 174.5 percent (from 2.9 million to 7.9 million). In Nigeria, the number increased by 53.5 percent (from 761,645 to 1.1 million), and in India, by 54.8 percent (from 5.9 million to 9.1 million).

The same happened with the number of students in Catholic universities and institutes, which is growing even more at the global level, by 54.4 percent. Unlike in schools, the majority of these students are no longer in Europe, but in the Americas and especially in Asia, where there are more students in Catholic universities than in Europe.

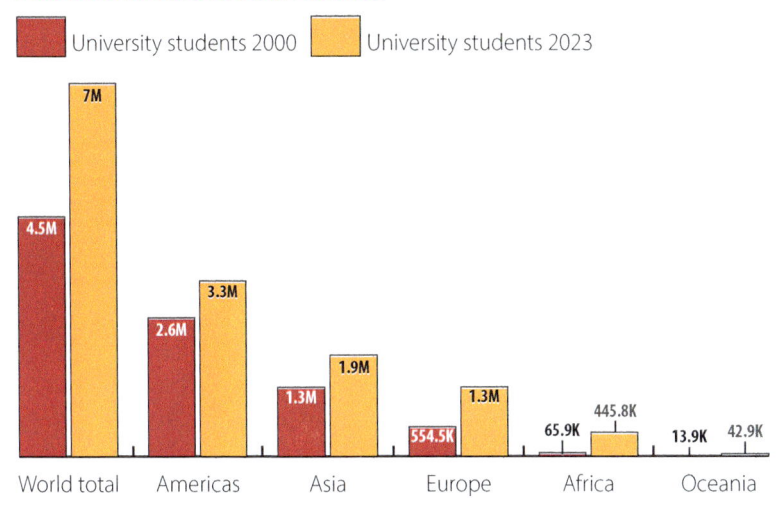

Students in Catholic Universities

■ University students 2000   ■ University students 2023

- World total: 4.5M (2000), 7M (2023)
- Americas: 2.6M, 3.3M
- Asia: 1.3M, 1.9M
- Europe: 554.5K, 1.3M
- Africa: 65.9K, 445.8K
- Oceania: 13.9K, 42.9K

Source: Statistical Yearbook of the Church 2000 and 2023

The United States has the largest number of students in Catholic universities, and their number continues to grow: 44.2 percent (from 892,100 in 2000 to 1.2 million in 2023). The country with the second largest number of students in Catholic universities is India, with a growth in this period of 132.7 percent (from 363,900 to 846,649).

The number of university students also increased by 85.9 percent in Brazil (from 330,636 to 614,475) and by 15 percent in Mexico (from 189,144 to 217,479).

There is an impressive increase in the number of students in higher education institutions in the Democratic Republic of Congo: In 2000 they were only 7,467, while in 2023 they reached 77,178, an increase of 933.6 percent; in Nigeria, this increase was 65.8 percent (from 17,573 to 29,137).

The geographical shift in Catholic educational institutions is significant when comparing schools and universities. In the first case, Africa accounts for 44.9 percent of students, while in higher education, 47 percent are enrolled in the Americas. In both cases, the percentage of students in Asia is higher than in Europe.

Students in Catholic Schools vs. Students in Catholic Universities and Higher Institutes

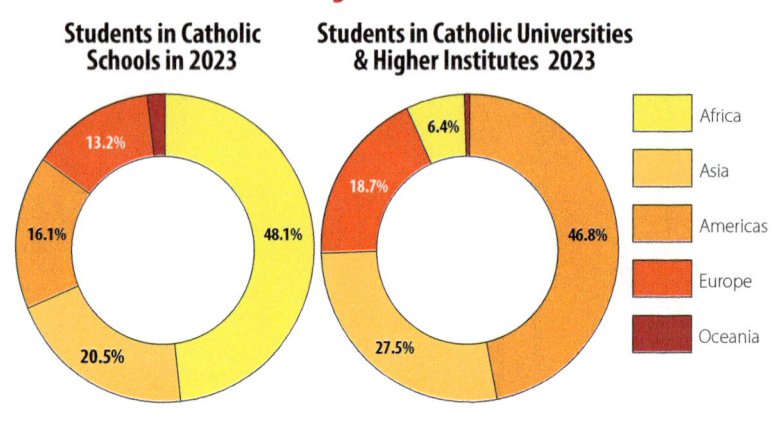

Students in Catholic Schools in 2023
- 48.1%
- 20.5%
- 16.1%
- 13.2%

Students in Catholic Universities & Higher Institutes 2023
- 46.8%
- 27.5%
- 18.7%
- 6.4%

Legend: Africa, Asia, Americas, Europe, Oceania

Source: Statistical Yearbook of the Church 2000 and 2023

The World's Largest Aid Organization

The Catholic Church is the institution that has created and manages the largest number of charitable institutions. In the world there are 103,951 Catholic hospitals; dispensaries; leprosaria; homes for the elderly, chronically ill, invalids, and handicapped; orphanages; nursery schools; marriage counseling centers; and special centers for social education or reeducation. This is an increase of 0.5 percent from 2000, when there were 103,417 such Catholic-run institutions.

Welfare Institutions

Legend: Welfare institutions 2000 | Welfare institutions 2023

Region	2000	2023
World total	103.4K	104K
Americas	36.4K	32.9K
Europe	30.8K	38.5K
Asia	20.5K	16.6K
Africa	14.2K	13.9K
Oceania	1.5K	2.1K

Source: Statistical Yearbook of the Church 2000 and 2023

Challenges and Signs of Hope

This analysis of the numbers of the Catholic Church in the world allows us to understand more objectively and globally both the challenges and the signs of hope facing Christianity in general, and Catholicism in particular, as we approach the third millennium of the redemption.

In the next two chapters, we will embark on a journey to discover the lights and shadows of Catholicism that, from every continent, looks to the leadership that Pope Leo XIV is called to exercise. These factors will mark the agenda of his pontificate.

Chapter 6

The Challenges Facing the Catholic Church Today

The numbers in the preceding chapter show that the Catholic Church faces enormous challenges across the globe in this epochal change. Will Pope Leo be able to overcome these challenges and shine light on the shadows? Could the Catholic Church collapse due to the impact of increasing secularization or its own internal decline? Let us seek together the answer to these pressing questions.

A Schism in the Church?

The biggest and most urgent challenge Leo XIV faces as pope is that of mending the splits in the Catholic Church. Some people believe these divisions could lead to a breakup within the Church — a schism.

A schism in the Church refers to a major division or split within the Church, in which a group of Catholics breaks away and separates itself from the authority and communion of the pope and the rest of the Catholic Church. There are two main kinds of schism. Formal schism occurs when a group intentionally and formally establishes a separate church or ecclesial community that is no longer in communion with the pope, as has happened with the Orthodox Churches, Anglicanism, and Protestantism more generally.

There are also informal schisms, which occur when there is a significant division or disagreement among the members of the Church, but which have not led to a formal schism or the establishment of a separate Church. They occur when Catholics refuse to submit to the authority of the pope or reject certain teachings of the Church, although outwardly they remain part of the Church.

Since the Church is to be "one, holy, catholic, and apostolic," schisms are the gravest sin against the unity that Christ intended for his followers. A schism is a denial of the desire expressed by Jesus at the Last Supper before his death: "That they may all be one, as you, Father, are in me and I in you, that they also may be in us, that the world may believe that you sent me" (Jn 17:21).

The unity of the Church is the *raison d'être* of Pope Leo. The Code of Canon Law, in the second paragraph of canon 333, explains that the authority of the pope is precisely aimed at achieving "communion with the other bishops and with the universal Church." For the Catholic Church, unlike the rest of the Christian churches, the authority of the pope has ensured visible unity in its two thousand years of history. From a sociological point of view, it can be said that the central figure of the pope is the Church's great strength, which at the same time can become its great fragility.

The tremendous political, ideological, and social polarization that characterizes societies today has also had a strong impact on the Catholic community, which is why the Church is experiencing one of its greatest crises of unity in recent centuries.

The pontificate of Pope Francis, who with his evangelical roots has tried to show how the Church welcomes all people with open arms without judging their lives or behaviors, has generated open controversy within Catholic sectors.

The highest point of this division was reached with the publication of the declaration of the Dicastery for the Doctrine of the Faith, approved by Pope Francis on December 18, 2023, *Fiducia Supplicans*, "on the pastoral meaning of blessings," in which he opens "the possibility of blessing couples in irregular situations and same-sex couples without officially validating their status or changing in any way the Church's perennial teaching on marriage."

The document has received an unprecedented response from bishops (and even bishops' conferences), who have asked their priests not to give these blessings to couples in irregular situations, as suggested in the Vatican declaration.

The Synod of Bishops on Synodality, whose final assembly was held in the Vatican in October 2024, also raised fears of schism in some circles because of its discussion of issues that cause deep divisions within the Church, such as the ordination of women to the priesthood, the ordination of married men to the priesthood, and the female diaconate.

In order to avoid dividing the Church, on March 14, 2024, Pope Francis removed the most controversial topics from the debate of this synodal assembly and left them in the hands of expert groups that were to offer their conclusions in 2025, allowing the synod to focus on its central topic: How to transform the Catholic Church into a more inclusive, participatory, and mission-oriented community?

Another phenomenon that has raised fears of schism in the Catholic Church is the "synodal way" promoted by the Church in Germany, particularly due to the controversial proposals it has attempted to implement for the Church in the country, against the will of the Vatican. Faced with the disastrous handling of sexual abuse by the bishops, this assembly studied the possibility of taking power away from the bishops and giving it to the laity. Such a proposal provoked a backlash from the Vatican.

But the current divisions in the Church do not only concern synods or the Catholic hierarchy. The discussion forums on social networks often show a high degree of aggressiveness. At times, ideological hatred characterizes the tone of the followers of Jesus Christ on the internet. This is a real scandal that alienates many people from the Church. "If Catholics argue about important issues of faith and life, how can you expect me to follow them?" is the most common comment. This is sadly a far cry from the "see how they love each other" that led the pagans of the Roman Empire to convert to Christianity.

Christ left his disciples with love as the greatest commandment, yet many Catholics engage in verbal violence, supposedly in the interests of defending the Church or the Truth. These divisions among Catholics are one of the serious reasons for the loss of credibility in the Church today.

In short, only a united Church can proclaim the Gospel of Jesus Christ on the two thousandth anniversary of the Redemption, and that is a huge challenge for Pope Leo XIV. A fractious and divided Church is not credible. This means that Leo XIV's pontificate must work tirelessly to find common ground on controversial issues, appealing to the fundamental principles of Sacred Scripture and Catholic Tradition that unite all the faithful, regardless of their different sensitivities.

The Scandal of Scandals

Clearly, Pope Leo inherits from his predecessors the task of confronting and eradicating clergy sexual abuse and abuses of power and conscience within the Catholic Church. This is one of the greatest challenges the Church has faced since these scandals came to light in the 1990s.

The victims of these abuses, the vast majority of whom were minors and vulnerable people, have suffered devastating psychological, physical, and spiritual trauma with lifelong consequences. The harshest words of the Gospel are addressed by Jesus to those who harm the little ones: "Whoever causes one of these little ones who believe in me to sin, it would be better for him to have a great millstone hung around his neck and to be drowned in the depths of the sea" (Mt 18:6).

The consequences of these scandals are before everyone's eyes. They have seriously eroded the trust and credibility of the faithful in the official representatives of the Church. Some disappointed believers have even chosen to leave the Church because of these scandals.

The reputation of the Church as an institution has been severely damaged in the eyes of the public, as in many cases it has been seen as covering up crimes and lacking transparency in its handling of abuse cases. As the hypocrisy and misdeeds of some clergy have been revealed, the authority of the Church to teach on moral issues and values has been undermined.

The scandal of scandals occurred with the cover-up of the abuses. Hostage to an actual heresy that sought to present all pastors as holy and perfect, abuses were too often covered up. The solution lies not only in the strict observance of protocols, but also in overcoming this false and disembodied image of a holy and perfect Church, which was able to justify the unjustifiable.

These scandals have caused divisions and polarization within the Church. Often, "conservatives" and "progressives" have tried to interpret the causes of this cancer according to their own parameters and have lobbied for solutions to support a particular ideological agenda, ultimately forgetting about the root causes that underlie these failings and unintentionally ignoring the issue's most dramatic and lasting aftermath, which is the ongoing suffering of the victims.

Despite the efforts of Francis and Benedict XVI to address these cases, repair the damage, and establish stricter protocols, the Church continues to face the effects of the crisis. Regaining trust and credibility will take much time, as well as maximum transparency. Doubts continue to be raised about the handling of cases such as those of Marko Ivan Rupnik, Theodore McCarrick, or, years ago, Marcial Maciel.

Will Pope Leo XIV finally be able to turn the page on the Church's consistent response to sexual abuse? The answer to that question may in large part determine the balance of his pontificate.

The Decrease of Religious Practice

The ongoing decrease of religious practice clearly poses a challenge for Pope Leo XIV. The Church is not a nongovernmental organization. After all, when it offers the sacraments and prayer, it does so to help cultivate a life of loving relationship with God.

When bishops, priests, and committed Catholics see the decrease of the faithful in churches, they tend to condemn their brothers and sisters, criticizing them for "living in a world as if God did not exist." Now, this does not mean that people are not seeking God. It means that they are not finding him in the Church. More people today, especially in Western societies, identify as nonreligious, atheist, agnostic, or with no religious affiliation.

We are thus witnessing the phenomenon of the privatization of religion, where religion is increasingly seen as a personal and private matter, rather than having a positive public influence on laws, policies, and social life.

The false opposition between science and faith in God has led to a rejection of religion, especially among younger generations. This phenomenon suggests that the loss of faith is often linked to a lack of Christian formation among the faithful. This raises the question of the role of Catholic parishes, schools, and universities in a post-Christendom society.

A separate issue is the lack of spiritual nourishment provided by parish life and, specifically, by the priests' homilies at Mass. In surveys and discussion forums, poor homilies are often cited by ex-Catholics as one of the reasons they became disillusioned with their parish experience and eventually left. Young people, especially, have expressed frustration with uninspired, irrelevant sermons that fail to engage them spiritually or intellectually.

Post-Christendom poses a pressing question for the pontificate of Leo XIV: Can the Church continue to base primary evangelization on access to the sacraments? Can contemporaries approach the Christian faith directly through the sacraments, as was often the case in the time of Christendom? Are the sacraments a way of arrival rather than a starting point?

The sacraments require a prior preparation and understanding of the Catholic Faith, which is lacking in those who do not have a minimal catechetical foundation. This is what Pope St. John Paul II and Pope Benedict XVI referred to with the term "new evangelization" — that is, evangelization that should not be new in its message, but in the methods and language of sharing it. What methods or expressions might better deliver the message is still to be discovered in most parishes today.

Disagreement with the Moral Teachings of the Church

Another of the great challenges of post-Christendom is the disagreement of the faithful with the moral teachings of the Church, especially those concerning the sexual sphere. This is a crucial question because it touches the most intimate aspects of the person. There is a common joke among parish priests that the faithful care less about whether there are three or four persons in the Trinity than they do about with whom and when they can have sexual relations.

This question has been particularly open since the publication of the encyclical *Humanae Vitae* by Pope St. Paul VI in 1968 in which he addressed issues related to contraception as well as the defense of the unborn child in the face of recourse to abortion.

A particularly symbolic moment that marked the advancing end of Christendom took place in the first week of March 2024, when the "firstborn daughter" of the Church, France, under intense pressure from its president, Emmanuel Macron, and with the approval of the National Assembly (780 votes in favor and 70 against), proclaimed abortion as a human right recognized by the French constitution. What the Church considers to be the worst injustice that can be committed against an unborn child, who is totally unprotected, is promoted by the state as a fundamental constitutional right.

The Christian vision of marriage as a lifelong commitment, sealed by God, clashes with the great number of broken marriages among the Catholic faithful, even among people involved in parish life or ecclesial movements. The drama of divorce is often a cause of a person's definitive rupture with the Church.

In recent years, another debate within the Catholic community has focused on the issue of homosexuality and related gender issues. On the one hand, thanks to the *Catechism of the Catholic Church*, published with the approval of John Paul II in 1992, ecclesial communities have come to understand the importance of welcoming homosexual persons. "They must be accepted with respect, compassion, and sensitivity," the *Catechism* states (2358).

On the other hand, the pontificate of Pope Francis, while confirming the teaching of the same *Catechism* that "homosexual acts are intrinsically disordered" (2357), has warned against the sin of pride of those who judge another person, as Jesus repeatedly explains in the Gospel (see Jn 8:7, Mt 7:1–5, Lk 6:37).

Even today, in the heart of the Church, there are enormous and ongoing debates trying to pinpoint where the red line is between the welcome and appreciation that LGBTQ+ people deserve as children of God, and a pastoral care for these people that can end up promoting or morally justifying all kinds of sexual relationships. In any case, we must note that this argument has been another reason for many people leaving the Church.

Regarding the end of life, the Church holds that euthanasia and assisted suicide, as opposed to palliative care, are morally wrong because they involve the intentional taking of a human life. Many countries, even those of Catholic tradition, have legalized euthanasia. The next step, which some, including France with Emmanuel Macron, are publicly proposing, is to establish euthanasia as a human right enshrined in the constitution.

The challenge of Leo XIV's pontificate will be to overcome a great misunderstanding of hundreds of years: that Christianity is simply about rules and ideology. "Being Christian is not the result of an ethical choice or a lofty idea, but the encounter with an event, a person, who gives life a new horizon and a decisive direction," wrote Pope Benedict XVI in his encyclical *Deus Caritas Est*.[24] Christianity, then, consists in the encounter with Jesus Christ, not in whether one is "conservative" or "progressive."

In the face of structural opposition to the Catholic position on numerous grounds, Pope Leo XIV will place three words at the center of Christianity: "God is love" (1 Jn 4:8). This simple but powerful statement will guide the new pope in his mission. This means welcoming everyone, listening to their stories, and understanding that each person is on a unique spiritual journey. Empathy and compassion are not only powerful tools for healing divisions, they are fundamental to living out the Gospel. This is where Jesus' teaching to "love your neighbor as yourself" (Mk 12:31) becomes critical. This means approaching people with understanding and respect, even when there is disagreement.

Social Justice and Ecology

The commandment of love is also the reason why Catholics not only engage in works of charity but also work for profound social justice on behalf of their brothers and sisters. While canon law prevents clerics from entering politics, in the case of lay Catholics, social, economic, and political involvement is considered "a lofty vocation and one of the highest forms of charity, inasmuch as it seeks the common good."[25]

The first encyclical highlighting the social doctrine of the Church, *Rerum Novarum*, was written by Pope Leo XIII in 1891. It addressed the conditions of the working class, criticizing both unbridled capitalism and socialism and defending the rights and dignities of workers, including the right to form unions and to just compensation.

The pontificate of Francis, which contributed the encyclicals *Laudato Si'* (May 24, 2015) and *Fratelli Tutti* (October 3, 2020), and the apostolic exhortation *Laudate Deum* (October 4, 2023), specifically addressed two of the great emergencies facing humanity today: the challenge of human migration and the ecological crisis.

On some of these issues, Jorge Mario Bergoglio took firm positions on highly sensitive matters that did not always enjoy the consensus of all Catholic sensibilities. In fact, in general, many of the issues of social justice are not arguments that are part of the essence of the Faith, which is why they are open to the legitimate sensibilities and opinions of the faithful.

Pope Leo XIV will therefore have a dual challenge: First and foremost, to illuminate in the light of faith the evolution of the great planetary challenges, including migrations; the impact of new technologies on human life, particularly biotechnology and artificial intelligence; employment justice in a hyper-connected and hyper-technological society; as well as respect for creation (which is part of the beginning of the profession of faith of the Christian creed itself).

On the other hand, he may have to promote a new synthesis of Christian social doctrine to stimulate Catholic reflection, separating issues that depend on the legitimate opinion and sensitivity of each person or group from those that constitute the very heart of the Christian social message based on the teachings of Jesus Christ and the Tradition of the Church.

Chapter 7

SIGNS OF HOPE

---✠---

Curiously, in the great challenges the Church faces today, there are also implicit signs of hope. The signs of the times are ambivalent; they are generally real dangers that can become opportunities. They refer to significant events, trends, and developments in the world that can reveal the presence or absence of God's work, and which the Church is called to discern and interpret in the light of the Gospel.

The biblical term "signs of the times" was introduced into the Magisterium by Pope St. John XXIII in the apostolic constitution of convocation of the Second Vatican Council, *Humanae Salutis*. In that document, he declared: "We renew our confidence in our Savior who has not left the world he redeemed. Instead we make our own the recommendation that one should know how to distinguish the *signs of the times* (Mt 16:3), and we seem to see now in the midst of so much darkness a few indications that argue well for the fate of the Church and humanity."[26]

For this reason, the challenges facing the Church, which we examined in Chapter 6, implicitly become signs of hope if we apply true evangelical discernment and a coherent pastoral strategy. In this sense, the current crisis that the Church is experiencing in post-Christendom times — a crisis of power, of social influence, of loss of the faithful and vocations — can become a real opportunity.

The young priest Joseph Ratzinger predicted this better than anyone else in an address to the German radio station Hessischer Rundfunk, broadcasted Christmas Day 1969, in which he predicted a totally resized Catholic Church for the third Christian millennium: a minority Church, politically not very influential, socially irrelevant, but a much more evangelical Church, learning humility through humiliation, a Church forced to start anew.

The "Forgotten Prophecy" of the Young Ratzinger

Ratzinger's intervention was later described by several media outlets as the "forgotten prophecy," when it was published in English by Ignatius Press in the book *Faith and the Future* (2009). These words of the future Pope Benedict XVI constitute an analysis of how the great problems and challenges we face today are "signs of hope."

Father Ratzinger explained before the radio microphone:

> From the crisis of today the Church of tomorrow will emerge — a Church that has lost much. She will become small and will have to start afresh more or less from the beginning. She will no longer be able to inhabit many of the edifices she built in prosperity. As the number of her adherents diminishes, so it will lose many of her social privileges. In contrast to an earlier age, it will be seen much more as a voluntary society, entered only by free decision.[27]

Ratzinger invites believers to go a step further:

> The Church will be a more spiritual Church, not presuming upon a political mandate, flirting as little with the left as with the right. It will be hard going for the Church, for the process of crystallization and clarification will cost her much valuable energy. It will make her poor and cause her to become the Church of the meek. The process will be all the more arduous, for sectarian narrow-mindedness as well as pompous self-will have to be shed.

Joseph Ratzinger concluded his radio reflection with these words: "The Catholic Church will survive in spite of men and women, not necessarily because of them. And yet, we still have our part to do. We must pray for and cultivate unselfishness, self-denial, faithfulness, sacramental devotion, and a life centered on Christ."[28]

Being a Christian: An Increasingly Conscious Decision

The first conclusion that can be drawn from Ratzinger's reflection is that in our post-Christendom, postmodern times, many people, especially pastors and the faithful who are deeply committed to the Church, could wring their hands over the clear abandonment of so many of the faithful.

On the other side of the coin, however, there is good news. Religiosity among Christians is becoming more and more authentic and personal and not merely established or social. Thus, by transforming people into their best selves, religion becomes more credible and desirable.

Baptism, in so many families in the West, is no longer a practice dictated by family or social tradition. The global collapse in the number of baptisms and couples celebrating the Sacrament of Matrimony in the Church speaks for itself. It is becoming increasingly clear that to be Christian, to be Catholic, is a choice that goes against the grain in terms of the freedom and faith of the family, or the person concerned.

The percentage of adult baptisms in the Catholic Church is increasing every year. Worldwide, 14.8 percent of those baptized in 2000 were over the age of seven, while in 2023 that percentage reached 20.5 percent, according to the Church's Statistical Yearbook.

Faced with the decline in the baptism of infants, the baptism of adults has become a phenomenon in European countries with a majority Catholic tradition. The most emblematic case is that of France. In 2024, the Catholic Church in the country experienced a significant increase in baptisms among adults and young people. Approximately 12,000 individuals were baptized during the Easter Vigil, comprising about 7,000 adults and over 5,000 teenagers aged eleven to seventeen. This represents a 31 percent increase compared to the previous year.

In some dioceses, the numbers have doubled. The proportion of young adults between the ages of eighteen and twenty-five has grown particularly rapidly, increasing by 150 percent in the last five years. People who were raised without religion account for nearly a quarter of the newly baptized. About 5 percent of these new Christians come from a Muslim background.

To a lesser extent, the same phenomenon is occurring in other European countries such as Spain and Belgium, where the coexistence of people of different religions and atheists increasingly characterizes the life of Catholics due to immigration.

Here we see a clear challenge for the pontificate of Leo XIV. It is true that Catholicism has become a minority in post-Christendom, but it is up to him to do everything possible to make it a "creative minority" — that is, to animate the hearts of the faithful with authentic motives of faith, hope, and Christian charity. Ours must be a Christianity of the convinced, not of the sociable.

Blood of Martyrs

We Catholics in the West are so wrapped up in our own problems that we forget that religious persecution in the world is now at an absolute record high.

In his address to the diplomatic corps accredited to the Holy See on January 9, 2023, Pope Francis denounced, based on public reports, "that one out of every seven Christians experiences persecution." This statement was confirmed by an informative note published the following day by Aid to the Church in Need, a Catholic charity serving persecuted Christians worldwide since 1947.

This organization, which publishes an annual "Religious Freedom Report," stated in 2023:

> Globally, the retention and consolidation of power in the hands of autocrats and fundamentalist group leaders led to increased violations of all human rights, including religious freedom. A combination of terrorist attacks, destruction of religious heritage and symbols (Turkey, Syria), electoral system manipulation (Nigeria, Iraq), mass surveillance (China), proliferation of anti-conversion laws and financial restrictions (Southeast Asia and Middle East) increased the oppression of all religious communities.[29]

The situation of Christians in the world is increasingly difficult, as the report notes:

> Occurring mostly without protest, governments applied controversial laws restricting freedom of religion or discriminated against certain religious communities (anti-conversion laws). At the same time, violent attacks against those of the "wrong" religion were "normalized" and mostly not prosecuted (Latin America). This was also observed in Western nations but there was better recourse to justice.[30]

It is estimated that the largest number of Christians killed throughout the world at this time are in Nigeria. Meanwhile, when asked the question, "Apart from weddings, funerals, and christenings, how often do you attend religious services these days?" 94 percent of self-identified Nigerian Catholics surveyed said they attend weekly or daily Mass.

Is this not a sign of hope for Christianity?

Pope Leo XIV has a surprisingly little-acknowledged ally: the witness of millions of persecuted Christians capable of facing social, political, and economic marginalization, or even death itself, in order to be consistent with their faith. It is a matter of finding a way to give a voice to these persecuted people so that their example may become, even today, a "seed of new Christians."

Awakening of the "Sleeping Giant"

The third millennium will be the awakening of the "sleeping giant" in the Church — that is, the laity, as predicted by American professor and diplomat Mary Ann Glendon in an article published in the November 2002 issue of *First Things* magazine under the title, "The Hour of the Laity."

"For decades, the giant has seemed lost in the deep slumber of an adolescent. Now that the sleeper is beginning to stir — roused by media coverage of clerical sexual misconduct — it is beginning to look as though the Leviathan has the faith I.Q. of a preadolescent. Can this be the long-awaited 'hour of the laity'?" wondered Glendon, who represented Pope St. John Paul II at the United Nations summit on women in 1995.

It is normal for the faithful to be overwhelmed by the decline in priestly vocations in the West. However, we lose sight of the fact that the Church is living a historic moment with the new responsibility of the laity in the work of evangelization.

As mentioned above, in some countries lay missionaries are changing the Catholic fabric. They are now more numerous than priests. The number of catechists is 2,866,966, more than twice the number of priests, nuns, and bishops combined.

The Catholic Church, like individuals, slowly learns from its own mistakes and difficulties. The profession of faith, the Creed, was often defined in response to doctrinal errors (heresies) that arose among some of the faithful in the early centuries. Similarly, the crisis of sexual abuse by members of the clergy, as many experts have explained, has among its various causes a false clericalism that has characterized important periods in the history of Catholicism.

According to Pope Francis, clericalism refers to a kind of "ecclesiastical narcissism," as well as a club mentality and a system of nepotism in which bishops and priests attribute to themselves privileges and decisions in areas that are not their own, and which correspond to the proper responsibility of the Christian faithful by virtue of their baptism.

Pope Leo XIV will also have to guide the Church in the current discernment to effectively understand the true role that women are called to play in the Church. In general, there is a broad consensus among the Catholic community and the hierarchy on the need to make more room for women in the Church. Problems and divisions arise when faced with the question of how to do this.

In the pontificate of Francis, some steps have been taken to give women responsibility in the Roman Curia and to open the ministries of lector and acolyte in the liturgy to women in a stable and institutionalized way. For the first time, women have been appointed to head important departments of the Holy See and Vatican City.

The study group created by Pope Francis during the Synod on Synodality on "the necessary participation of women in the life and leadership of the Church" is currently working. The results should be made public in 2025.

Christian families are seen by many as one of the great hopes of the Catholic Church in the post-Christendom era, precisely because they are considered "domestic churches." Christian families, despite their limits and imperfections, are signs in the world of the presence of God in the postmodern age, as was the case in the time of the Roman Empire.

Chapter V of the Letter to Diognetus, written between AD 130 and 200, describes in an apologetic tone, but no less significantly, the life of the Christians of the Roman Empire who evangelized the known world at that time:

> They live in their own countries as though they were only passing through. They play their full role as citizens, but labor under all the disabilities of aliens. Any country can be their homeland, but for them their homeland, wherever it may be, is a foreign country. Like others, they marry; they beget children; but they do not destroy their offspring. They share their meals, but not their wives.

The letter continues:

> They live in the flesh, but they are not governed by the desires of the flesh. They pass their days upon earth, but they are citizens of heaven. Obedient to the laws, they yet live on a level that transcends the law. Christians love all men, but all men persecute them. Condemned because they are not understood, they are put to death but raised to life again. They live in poverty, but enrich many; they are totally destitute, but possess an abundance of everything. They suffer dishonor, but that is their glory.

Today's pontiff has the challenge of concretizing the process promoted by the Synod of Bishops on the future of the church to seek a more synodal Church, in which the voice of all its members is heard and valued, and in which each member assumes his or her responsibility as a baptized person. The concept of synodality has been difficult to understand for those not accustomed to theological language, but it is an authentic sign of hope for a Church that seeks to be more participatory in its mission in the postmodern world.

Spiritual Thirst of the Youth

As we said above, the signs of hope for the Church are also its great dangers. This is clearly seen among young people. While their belonging to the Church is inarguably diminishing, their thirst for spirituality is growing all over the world.

In societies that offer young people money and consumerism as the only horizon for their lives, a worldwide survey conducted by the GAD3 institute of sociological studies (a Spanish polling group) for the Pontifical University of the Holy Cross, together with seven other universities from around the world, and presented in Rome on February 29, 2024, found that young people are increasingly interested in spirituality.[31]

The study, conducted among 4,889 men and women between the ages of eighteen and twenty-nine in Argentina, Brazil, Spain, the

Philippines, Italy, Kenya, Mexico, and the United Kingdom, shows that among these young people, spirituality is "not at all present" in 6 percent, "somewhat present" in 19 percent, "quite present" in 29 percent, and "very present" in 44 percent.

Among the most noteworthy results of the research was the presence of a significant minority of young people who are Catholics "by conviction": Catholics who live their faith with authenticity, replacing the "socio-cultural" religion — that is, the one lived by mere tradition. This trend is more pronounced in countries that have been in the midst of a de-Christianization process for years — countries such as Spain and Italy — the study concludes.

St. John Paul II had the brilliant idea of showing young Catholics that they are not alone when he convened the first World Youth Day, and which continued every couple of years and broke participation records in the history of Christianity. In a world where the number of these young people has decreased, even as their Christian commitment has increased, the new pope will have to find ways to show today's young people that they are not alone, even when it seems that their whole lives are spent rowing against the tide of society.

Secularization Is Reaching Its Limit

This analysis seems to suggest that the advance of secularization is inexorable. However, in some countries, signs are beginning to emerge that indicate secularization is reaching its peak. This is another sign of hope. Secularization offers no answers to the great questions of life, and it is precisely at this point that Christianity returns with its full force and compelling message.

This is the conclusion reached by Bishop Erik Varden, OCSO, of Trondheim in Norway, Trappist monk, who also serves as the president of the Scandinavian Bishops' Conference. He believes that secularization has reached its limit in the region. "People are not satisfied," he explains. "Interest in Christianity and in fundamental questions about human nature and the purpose of life is growing."

"The radical secularization of the past few decades has caused widespread forgetfulness — it takes no more than a generation and a half for a residual religious identity to fade," underlines the Scandinavian bishop. "When I grew up in the '80s, most people thought they knew what Christianity was. That is no longer the case, and there is no embarrassment associated with ignorance."

"This is a cultural loss," Bishop Varden continues. "At the same time, it is an advantage for evangelization. For now, it is possible to present the Gospel in its freshness, and for it to be perceived as new and alive. We have a great task before us — both demanding and joyful. It has several aspects that must be developed simultaneously."

He concluded, "We need to find ways to communicate authentic Catholic teaching; we must teach people to pray, allowing them to discover the richness of the liturgy; we must show that Catholics have constructive and attractive contributions to make in politics and culture; and we must make our faith tangible through charitable work."

Even in the United States, signs of fatigue in the secularization process are becoming evident. After years of steady decline, the percentage of Americans identifying as Christians appears to be stabilizing — at least temporarily — at just over six in ten, according to a comprehensive new survey by the Pew Research Center, released February 26, 2025.[32]

According to the report, 44 percent of U.S. adults say they pray at least once a day. Though down significantly since 2007, this measure has held between 44 percent and 46 percent since 2021. Eighty-six percent believe people have a soul or spirit in addition to their physical body. Thirty-three percent say they go to religious services at least once a month. Since 2020, the percentages saying this have consistently hovered in the low 30s.

The survey throws up some interesting data that indicates how secularization has not been able to dry up the faith of Americans: 83 percent believe in God or a universal spirit; 79 percent believe there is something spiritual beyond the natural world; 70 percent believe in heaven, hell, or both.

"The Poor You Will Always Have with You"

Jesus Christ uttered a particularly enigmatic phrase in the Gospel of

Mark, when he stated: "The poor you will always have with you, and whenever you wish you can do good to them, but you will not always have me" (14:7). As we take part in the life of many parishes, prayer groups, or Catholic communities, we often come to realize that these words were profoundly prophetic.

The life of Christian communities today is made up of people who, according to the prevailing mentality, could be described as marginalized, poor, sick, and lonely. In fact, loneliness and marginalization are decisive factors for many people today when approaching the Church.

The post-Christendom age is giving rise to a Church that is poorer for the poor, and for this reason it is more credible, more humble. It is not only the people who knock on the doors of the Church to ask for food or concrete material assistance who discover the hidden riches of the Church. There are also many people with psychological problems or even mental illnesses who find a welcome and a listening ear in the Catholic community.

It should not be forgotten that, as we have shown in Chapter 5, the Catholic Church operates the largest charitable network in the world, with thousands of organizations providing food, shelter, health care, and other services to the poor worldwide.

Like the early Christians, Pope Leo XIV is called to invite the Church in postmodern times to be a "poor Church for the poor" and to prioritize service to the marginalized. Catholic social teaching emphasizes the "preferential option for the poor," which calls the Church to pay special attention to the needs of the poor and vulnerable.

The Acts of the Apostles provides numerous examples of the early Christian community's commitment to helping those in need. For example, Acts 2:44–45 and Acts 4:32–35 describe how the early Christians shared all they had, selling their possessions and goods and distributing the proceeds to anyone who was in need.

The Letter of James admonishes the Church for ignoring the needs of the poor among them, emphasizing that faith without works is dead (see 2:15–16). James 1:27 also defines "religion that is pure and undefiled before God" as caring for orphans and widows in their distress.

The *Didache*, an early Christian document, possibly from the late first or early second century, provides instructions on Christian ethics, rituals, and church organization. It includes exhortations to give to the poor and guidance on how to treat the community's possessions as if they belonged to the poor.

One of the reasons for hope in the future of the Church is based on the promise of Jesus: "You will always have the poor with you." The poor will always be with us to remind us of the true meaning of Christianity.

True Hope

All these signs of hope clearly show that the postmodern reality should not be seen only from a pessimistic and negative perspective, as Christians have often conceived it. Ours is rather an era of challenges and opportunities. It does force believers to change their mind-set, however. The future does not lie in returning to the security of a lost Christendom, but in living the challenge of the unknown, trusting in God's love.

The West, after the drift of materialism — the true cancer of our society — will eventually rediscover Christianity, and Jesus Christ, as the beacon of humanity. And perhaps it will even become Catholic, understanding this term in its literal sense — that is, universal. It cannot be otherwise, since Truth is one and inclusive. The West is ceasing to be Christian, and in particular Catholic, in name in order to become Christian — Catholic — in truth.

Chapter 8

Ten Messages Pope Leo XIV Carries in His Heart

---✠---

Robert Prevost is a man of his word, but he is not a man of many words. He has dedicated his ministry as a priest, a missionary, an Augustinian superior, and a bishop to serving those around him. He has not written any books, except for a doctoral thesis on canon law. He has not left behind any major documents. He has been a pastor with his words, but these have rarely been recorded.

For this reason, it has been necessary to research his homilies, speeches, and interviews in Peru and Rome to understand the issues that are close to his heart and what influence they will have on the universal Church during his pontificate. In this chapter, we will reflect on some of his most cherished thoughts.

1. "God Loves Us ... All of Us"

When a pontiff utters his first words after the announcement of "*Habemus Papam*" from the balcony of St. Peter's Basilica, he tries to concentrate on the message of his future pontificate. In a sense, he takes up the theme of his life and makes it a program.

Pope Leo summed it up in three words, "God loves us," and shortly thereafter added, "all of us." This powerful yet simple message, which challenges every person, sums up his life and his message.

"God loves us, God loves you all, and evil will not prevail!" assured the new pontiff in his first words as pope. "We are all in God's hands. Therefore, without fear, holding hands with God and with one another, let us move forward."

From the very beginning, Leo XIV presented himself as "a son of Saint Augustine," the saint born in North Africa in 354, known as the teacher of grace and love.

From the founder of the Augustinian order, Brother Prevost learned as a young man that God loves each person in his particularity, not in an abstract way. God does not love humanity as a mass, but each human being is the object of an intimate, personal, and unconditional love. "God loves each one of us as if there were no one else to love."[33]

Reading Saint Augustine's *Confessions* at the minor seminary of the Augustinian Fathers, Robert Francis Prevost discovered the secret of human happiness: "You have made us for yourself, Lord, and our hearts are restless until they rest in you."[34] During those early years as an Augustinian, the future pope discovered that God creates human beings with an innate vocation: to love and be loved by him. Every person bears this "restlessness" as a divine seal.

As Robert came to realize his desire to be a missionary in a distant country, he also came to understand that divine love is not earned by human merit but rather received freely: "Everything is grace." God always takes the initiative to love first, before any human merit.

For Saint Augustine, divine love is dynamic; it transforms the human heart, orienting it toward God and toward others. To love

Cardinals stand on the balconies of St. Peter's Basilica at the Vatican to watch Pope Leo XIV greet the crowd for the first time and as he gives his blessing *urbi et orbi* ("to the city and the world"). (CNS photo/Pablo Esparza, © 2025, USCCB. All rights reserved.)

God, according to Augustine, implies loving others, because when we discover that we are deeply loved by God, our natural response is to love our fellow human beings.

Prevost decided to become an Augustinian religious and a Catholic priest in order to live and transmit the maxim of his founder: "Love and do what you will: if you keep silent, you will keep silent with love; if you cry out, you will cry out with love; if you correct, you will correct with love; if you forgive, you will forgive with love. If you have love rooted in you, nothing but love will be your fruit."[35]

True love can become the root of our existence, as Prevost preached as a priest and bishop. If our actions arise from love, then, regardless of what we do — whether we remain silent, speak, correct, or forgive — we will live in accordance with our vocation, with our destiny, with happiness. Love is, in fact, the supreme guide for life.

Saint Augustine emphasizes that God's love is manifested in his mercy. God loves by forgiving: "God's mercy is greater than all our miseries put together."[36]

In short, Leo XIV, a disciple of Augustine, wants to announce to the world today through his pontificate that authentic happiness lies in discovering that we are fully loved by God, and that loving him and receiving his love is the ultimate meaning of existence.

2. Encountering Christ: The Heart of Christianity

Love for Christ is the reason why Robert Prevost left everything behind in Chicago to become a missionary. He has dedicated his life to evangelization — that is, to introducing others to Christ, the Person he encountered as a child in his home, among his parents and siblings, and who won his heart forever.

"I still consider myself a missionary. My vocation, like that of every Christian, is to be a missionary, to proclaim the Gospel wherever one is," he explained in an interview with *Vatican News* shortly after Pope Francis called him to Rome to be prefect of the Dicastery for Bishops. "Our first duty is to communicate the beauty and joy of knowing Jesus,"[37] he insisted in the same interview, underscoring that Christianity is, at its heart, an encounter with a Person.

This conviction is so important to the new pope that, in his first homily, in the Sistine Chapel on May 9, 2025, before the cardinals, he stated, "Even today, there are contexts in which Jesus, while appreciated as a man, is reduced to a kind of charismatic leader or superman, and this not only among nonbelievers, but also among many baptized Christians, who thus end up living, at this level, in a de facto atheism."

For this reason, for Prevost, this personal encounter with Christ is the very center of the Christian experience, the reason capable of transforming human life. As he explained in a homily delivered on the liturgical memorial of Saint Augustine on August 28, 2024, this encounter "leads him to understand that the God he sought far from himself is the God close to every human being, the God close to our hearts, more intimate to us than ourselves."[38]

Following the experience of his teacher, Saint Augustine, Prevost added in that homily that, thanks to the encounter with Christ, Christians "do not close themselves off as if they had already arrived, but continue on the journey. Because the restlessness of the search for truth, the search for God, becomes the restlessness to know him more and more and to go out of oneself to make him known to others."

Prevost's pastoral experience in Peru taught him that hearts are won not by theological complexity alone but by witnessing to the love of Christ. Christ is the center of all the "arguments" Prevost addresses: from moral teaching to social action. From his perspective, everything starts with the person and message of Jesus. Christianity, for him, is not a system of rules or an ideology. It is the great news that changes not only people's lives, but also the motive capable of creating fraternal communities.

"Our priority has to be to live the good news, to live the Gospel, to share the enthusiasm that can be born in our hearts and in our lives when we truly discover who Jesus Christ is," he explained in a September 29, 2023, interview published on the website of the Order of St. Augustine.[39]

3. Jesus Among Us: The Forms of His Presence

If Christianity consists in finding Jesus as the Person capable of giving meaning to existence, then a pressing question arises: How is it possible to have this personal experience? How is Jesus Christ present among us?

Bishop Prevost answered this question on June 14, 2020, in a homily delivered in the cathedral of his diocese, Chiclayo, Peru, on the Solemnity of Corpus Christi.[40]

First of all, it is possible to encounter and experience Christ personally "in prayer and in the liturgy," clarified the Augustinian bishop. "Christ is present in his Church who prays, because it is he who prays for us, prays in us, and to whom we pray: He prays for us as our Priest; he prays in us as our Head, and we pray to him as our God."

Second, he went on to explain, Jesus is "in his Church who exer-

Pope Leo XIV processes out of the Sistine Chapel after celebrating his first Mass as pope with the cardinals who elected him May 9, 2025. (CNS photo/Vatican Media, © Vatican Media)

cises works of mercy, not only because when we do good to one of his little brothers we do it to Christ himself, but also because it is Christ himself who performs these works through his Church, thus continually helping men with his divine charity."

Third, Christ is present in the Church. This presence is real

> in his Church who journeys and longs to reach the port of eternal life, because he dwells in our hearts through faith and spreads charity in them through the work of the Holy Spirit whom he has given us. He is also present in his Church who preaches, since the Gospel which she proclaims is the Word of God. ... He is present in his Church who rules and governs the people of God, since sacred power derives from

Christ. ... Moreover ... Christ is present in his Church who offers the sacrifice of the Mass in his name and administers the sacraments.

Finally, there is a "distinct" mode of Jesus' presence, "truly sublime." This is "the sacrament of the Eucharist, which is therefore, among the other sacraments, the sweetest in devotion, the most beautiful in intelligence, the most holy in content. ... In the Eucharist, Christ is truly present among us — and through his Body and Blood, he makes us all Church."

Prevost explained that, for this reason, "the Church lives from the Eucharist. This truth ... encapsulates the core of the mystery of the Church." It is "a great mystery, a mystery of mercy, a mystery of love."

"God's love knows no measure," concluded the bishop of Chiclayo. "St. Augustine says that 'the measure of love is love without measure.' To love without limits — this is how God loves us, and this is how God calls us to live — to share his love with others. It is his love that calls us, that unites us, that makes us one family, a love that creates the Church, the communion of love."

4. Unity in the Church

Unity in the Church, always threatened by divisions, is the priority of the new pope as Bishop of Rome and successor of St. Peter. Already when he was consecrated bishop in Peru, he chose as his motto "*In Illo uno unum*," a Latin expression that means, "In the one Christ we are one." This motto was taken from a sermon on Psalm 127 by Saint Augustine.

For Prevost, Christ is the source and foundation of the Church's unity. This unity is not simply organizational or institutional, but a spiritual and mystical reality that is manifested in the communion of believers with Christ and with one another.

Following on the teachings of Saint Paul, Saint Augustine teaches that the Church is the Body of Christ, and Christ is its Head. This image emphasizes that all members of the Church are united to one another through their relationship with Christ.

For Prevost, love is essential for maintaining the unity of the Church. Without love, there can be no true communion among believers. This underscores the importance of unity as a witness to the truth of the Gospel and to Christ's presence in the world.

Unity in the Church, he explained in his interview posted on the Augustinian website, "is a real challenge, especially when polarization has become the modus operandi in a society that, rather than seeking unity as a fundamental principle, goes instead from extreme to extreme."[41]

Moreover, he asserted:

> Ideologies have acquired greater power than the real experience of humanity, of faith, of the actual values we live by. Some misconstrue unity as uniformity: "You have to be the same as we are." No. This cannot be. Nor can diversity be understood as a way of living without criteria or order. ... When an ideology becomes master of my life, then I can no longer dialogue or engage with another person because I have already decided how things will be. I am closed to encounter and transformation cannot, as a result, take place. ... This obviously makes it very challenging to be Church, to be community, to be brothers and sisters.

From this perspective, we can understand why, in his first words as pope, he opened his heart to express his deepest desire: "We want to be a synodal Church, a Church that walks, a Church that always seeks peace, that always seeks charity, that always seeks to be close especially to those who suffer."

5. Evangelization: More Than Words

For Prevost, the Church is not and cannot become a club for the privileged. The Church opens her arms to everyone. The new pope had said in his interview on the Augustinian order's website that our mission has remained the same since Jesus told his followers, "Go therefore and make disciples of all nations, baptizing them in the name of the Father and of the Son and of the Holy Spirit, teaching them to observe all that I have commanded you" (Mt 28:19).

Central to Prevost's vision of evangelization is the power of authentic witness. Proclaiming Christ effectively requires more than words; it demands a life lived in conformity with the Gospel message. He believes the faithful should see in the Christian witness an "incentive" to embrace the Faith more fully. The credibility of the messenger, demonstrated through actions and attitudes, is indispensable for the message to be heard and received.

Cardinal Prevost's consistent focus on the joy and beauty of the Faith, combined with his deep-seated missionary identity, points toward an approach to evangelization rooted in attraction and personal encounter rather than solely obligation or doctrinal imposition. This vision is a legacy of previous pontificates.

It represents a clear continuation of a primary thrust of Pope Francis's pontificate, emphasizing the relational and experiential dimensions of Christian faith as the wellspring of missionary activity.

Pope Benedict XVI focused his teaching on Christianity as an encounter with a Person, "which gives life a new horizon and a decisive direction."[42]

Pope St. John Paul II had the genius, during his long pontificate, to launch the movement of the new evangelization in the Church.

Pope St. Paul VI is remembered for the profound conviction he expressed in these words: "Modern man listens more willingly to witnesses than to teachers, and if he does listen to teachers, it is because they are witnesses."[43]

Pope Leo XIV believes that this observation challenges all baptized persons, and in particular the pastors of the Church. In his interview with *Vatican News* shortly after becoming head of the Dicastery for Bishops, Cardinal Prevost said:

> We are often preoccupied with teaching doctrine, the way of living our faith, but we risk forgetting that our first task is to teach what it means to know Jesus Christ and to bear witness to our closeness to the Lord. This comes first: to communi-

cate the beauty of the Faith, the beauty and joy of knowing Jesus. It means that we ourselves are living it and sharing this experience.[44]

For Robert Prevost, being a Christian, being a priest, being a bishop means "proclaiming Jesus Christ and living the faith so that the faithful see in his witness an incentive for them to want to be an ever more active part of the Church that Jesus Christ himself founded. In just a few words: to help people come to know Christ through the gift of faith."[45]

6. Near to the Poor and Vulnerable

As a missionary, priest, and bishop, Robert Prevost has shown particular concern for the poor and vulnerable. However, it is impossible to understand his vision of poverty without approaching his spirituality as an Augustinian religious.

Following the teaching of Saint Augustine, Prevost believes that true poverty is not only material deprivation, but humility of heart. Evangelical poverty is living without attachment to possessions, recognizing dependence on God and opening oneself to others.

The example of Jesus inspires Augustinians to serve the most humble through a simple life. For this reason, Augustinians are a mendicant order — that is, they renounce personal possessions and live the ideal of almsgiving, which places them in the hands of Providence, to serve their brothers and sisters with evangelical humility.

In his last interview before being elected pope, following the death of Francis, Cardinal Prevost emphasized the importance of "a poor Church, who walks with the poor, who serves the poor," as well as "the importance of being close to those who suffer and of having the heart of Jesus Christ,"[46] referring explicitly to his predecessor's closeness to migrants and refugees.

"I believe that the message of the Gospel is much better understood from the experience of the poor, who have nothing, who try to live their faith and find everything in Jesus Christ," he said in that interview.

A life of poverty allowed Prevost to create a special bond with the poor in the impoverished regions of Peru where he lived, devoting par-

Pope Leo XIV waves to the crowd from the central balcony of St. Peter's Basilica at the Vatican as he leads, for the first time, the midday recitation of the *Regina Coeli* May 11, 2025. (CNS photo/Vatican Media, © Vatican Media)

ticular attention to the exploited, to immigrants (including Venezuelans), to refugees, and to victims of natural disasters and COVID-19.

In a speech delivered October 14, 2015, at the Catholic University of Santo Toribio de Mogrovejo, he considered that in his diocese of Chiclayo, the eradication of poverty was an indispensable requirement for promoting "sustainable, integral development that seeks the common good for each person in themselves, for all people today and tomorrow, and for nature, learning from the natural rhythms of creation."[47]

In that speech, Prevost called on social agents and every Christian to apply "human genius" well in order to "creatively innovate" actions that allow for inclusion and overcome inequality.

The Augustinian religious lives the preferential option for the poor, but not in an exclusive way. On March 27, 2015, in a speech to business leaders gathered at the Catholic University of Santo Toribio de Mogrovejo, he asked them to "do everything possible to create or maintain jobs with working conditions and participation that correspond to the just demands of today's workers, while also taking into account the possibilities of our country and region. For the criterion is that work should serve man, and that the entire economy should be at the service of man, and not the other way around."[48]

In a later speech delivered at the First Industrial Forum 2015, organized by the university, Bishop Prevost explained: "When we give something of ours to the poor, we may be restoring something that does not belong entirely to us. Saint Ambrose said: 'You do not give the poor from your own, but you give them back what is theirs. For what is common belongs to everyone, not just the rich. ... You are therefore paying a debt, not giving freely what you do not owe.'"[49]

The bishop concluded, "Life experience, in the light of the Gospel, has taught us that materialism prevents us from being free and gives way to bitterness, ending up condemning us to unhappiness."

7. Business, Politics, and Society in Service of the Common Good

Anyone who wants to get closer to Pope Leo XIV's thinking will discover that his option for the poor is not exclusive. His humanizing vision also emphasizes the importance of initiative and the ability to do business in order to promote community development — in particular, dignified and motivating work.

In a speech delivered at the Catholic University of Santo Toribio de Mogrovejo, he noted "a level of interdependence between business and society, where the actions of some inevitably have an impact on others, and that interdependence is the starting point we must take into account when planning commercial policies that harmoniously contribute to the achievement of the common good." The bishop explained:

On the one hand, there is the community, understood as

the space where a group of people with certain social and economic characteristics, among other aspects, interact with their own problems and desires to seek sustenance and development. On the other hand, there is the company, the entity that depends precisely on these people, who are the main asset they have to achieve their main goal: profitability.[50]

"But how can society be strengthened?" asked the bishop:

> Who helps it? Who looks after the interests and needs of these people who often do not have access to basic education, for example, or to water and sewage services? This is where a third fundamental actor comes in, the state, which sets the "rules of the game."… Part of the state's great social responsibility in this context is to promote public policies that regulate, guarantee, and harmonize … the development of society by building bridges that create paths for public and private investment.

For this reason, Bishop Prevost mentioned in his speech the "Creating Shared Value" proposal promoted by Michael Porter and Mark Kramer, which encourages "policies and practices that improve a company's competitiveness by helping to improve the economic and social conditions of the communities in which it operates. In other words, a space where everyone wins and which goes beyond social responsibility."[51]

The company and society, he concluded, need leaders who are not only capable of developing a business strategy that can achieve a unique positioning and a distinctive value chain that reflects it, but also leaders with "new skills and knowledge, with a deeper perspective and — above all — a much deeper understanding of society's needs. … This is a new form of economic success where society, business, and the state all win."[52]

8. The Family as a School of Generosity and Discernment

For Robert Prevost, the family is the place where everyone can be themselves and feel loved just as they are. He devoted much of his efforts as priest and bishop in Peru to supporting families, especially young families.

In a speech on October 14, 2015, at the Catholic University of Santo Toribio de Mogrovejo, he referred to the family as "a place of evangelical holiness." He added, "In it, we breathe the memory of generations and deepen the roots that allow us to go further."[53] It is the place of discernment, where we are educated to discover God's plan for our lives and to know how to accept it with confidence.

These comments surely arose, at least in part, from Prevost's memories of childhood and adolescence in his own family. In the interview he gave to RAI before his election as pope, he recalled how his vocation as a missionary and priest arose precisely within the Catholic home that his parents had created for him and his brothers.

For this reason, Prevost invited educators and social agents

> to develop participatory and inclusive strategies that allow the formation of young marriages to nestle in them the spirit of Christ and strengthen their roots; and of mature marriages to rekindle conjugal love that allows them to be witnesses of faith. Let us contribute to the development of policies that give concrete space to family life and legislation capable of defending and ensuring the minimum conditions necessary for families, especially those just starting out, to develop. The family is a place of gratuitousness, of discreet, fraternal, and supportive presence.[54]

This explains why, on May 9, in his first homily as pope, he referred to "the crisis of the family" as one of those wounds "from which our society suffers so much." This implies a vision of the family that, without renouncing the Christian ideal, seeks to welcome and accompany families in their diverse realities and fragilities.

In his ministry as bishop of Chiclayo, Prevost worked hard to defend the right to life of the unborn, participating in pro-life events such as the March for Life rally in Chiclayo in 2015, where he urged people to "defend human life at all times." He has also used his social media accounts to share messages highlighting the importance of protecting life beginning at conception.

Although his approach is pastoral and avoids a combative tone, his opposition to abortion is clear and consistent with the official teaching of the Church. This stance reflects his commitment to traditional Catholic values and his emphasis on defending the most vulnerable.

9. Protagonists in the Church: Women and the Laity

The vision of the Church as an authentic community, in which Christ is the head, leads Robert Prevost to emphasize the leading role played by women, young people, and laypeople in general.

Pope Leo XIV has actively supported the inclusion of women in leadership positions within the Church. As prefect of the Dicastery for Bishops, he praised Pope Francis's decision to appoint three women as members of this dicastery responsible for assisting the Bishop of Rome in the selection of pastors for dioceses.

During the Synod on Synodality in October 2023, Prevost warned against the danger of "clericalizing women." He considered that this is not the right solution and that it could create new challenges within the ecclesiastical structure. For this reason, he advocated for a synodal Church, where all the faithful, including laypeople and women, actively participate in the life and mission of the Church.

Leo XIV believes that synodality and co-responsibility are essential to address polarization within the Church and to foster a renewal guided by the Holy Spirit. In an interview shortly after he was made a cardinal, Prevost said, "If we learn to live our faith better and learn to invite and include others in the life of the Church, especially the young, some vocations will still come to us."[55]

On the other hand, Prevost thinks "we have to see the layperson as a layperson. It is one of the many gifts that has evolved over the last few years: discovering that they have a very important role in the Church." At the same time, he asserted, "The priesthood has, and will continue to have, a very important role in the life of the Church and of all believers."[56]

10. Saint Augustine: Father and Timeless Advisor

St. Augustine of Hippo is Pope Leo XIV's spiritual father. He confessed this in his first words after being elected pope. Since he was a teenager, he has been hooked on the spirituality of the North African saint (354–430), and, after the Bible, he quotes most frequently from the writings of Saint Augustine in his speeches and homilies.

Augustine was a philosopher and theologian capable of systematically integrating Greco-Roman thought with Christian revelation, showing the harmony between faith and reason. Through the teachings of Augustine, Pope Leo came to understand that faith does not deny reason but elevates it.

On the other hand, Pope Leo learned from Augustine the importance of interiority, as expressed in the saint's *Confessions*, a pioneering work in the history of autobiographoies: "You have made us for

Pope Leo XIV coat of arms. (© Vatican Media)

yourself, Lord, and our hearts are restless until they rest in you." Like Augustine, Robert Prevost understands that Christians not only believe, they question, seek, desire, suffer, and convert. The experience of God is deeply existential.

This is what drives humanity, and Augustine is a master of bringing the theology of history to life. In *The City of God*, he reinterprets the destiny of humanity not as a succession of empires, but as a struggle between two loves: "Two loves founded two cities: the love of God to the point of self-contempt, and the love of self to the point of contempt for God."

Augustine is the pioneer of the modern self. Long before the birth of modern philosophers such as Sigmund Freud, Michel de Montaigne, or Jean-Jacques Rousseau, Augustine had already written a spiritual and psychological autobiography. *Confessions* explore inner struggle, desire, sin, memory, time, and the soul. He was the first to say "I" in an introspective and deeply human way, foreshadowing modern consciousness.

For Pope Leo, Augustine is his teacher in the subject to which he has dedicated his life: grace and love. The saint understood that salvation is the work of God's free grace. This theology of grace has shaped our new pope's spiritual outlook, which focuses on trust, humility, and ongoing conversion.

On a more intimate and personal level, Pope Leo is passionate about Augustine's vision of the Church as a community of brothers and sisters:

> When I think of Saint Augustine, his vision and understanding of what it means to belong to the Church, one of the first things that springs to mind is what he says about how you cannot say you are a follower of Christ without being part of the Church. Christ is part of the Church. He is the head. ... Saint Augustine's teachings touch every part of life and help us to live in communion.[57]

Epilogue

"Without Fear"

---✢---

From the moment the election of Pope Leo XIV was announced, we confronted a question that weighs on the minds of many in the face of declining religious practice: Could the Catholic Church disappear?

What this book has attempted to provide is an investigation — guided by data rather than speculation — into whether Christianity, on a global scale, has truly spoken its final word.

As we've turned these pages, we've uncovered signs of resilience and reasons for hope. More importantly, we've seen that every crisis brings with it a hidden opportunity. The widespread sense of meaninglessness that afflicts so many today, often condemning them to loneliness, is in fact a cry for meaning — a cry that challenges both Christians and the Church to respond with renewed courage and love.

In this context, the election of Robert Francis Prevost — the first American pope — as successor to the apostle Peter arrives like a breath of fresh air. His elevation was a surprise to the world. And his first words as pope came like healing balm:

> God loves us, God loves you all, and evil will not prevail! All of us are in God's hands. So, let us move forward, without fear, together, hand in hand with God and with one another! We are followers of Christ. Christ goes before us. The world needs his light. Humanity needs him as the bridge that can lead us to God and his love.

To the skeptics who predicted a Church fractured and void of direction, the conclave responded with the surprising figure of a missionary, a man who has reignited faith and spiritual vitality in places as far apart as the United States, Peru, and Cuba. Pope Leo XIV stands as living proof that Christianity is not ending; it is only beginning anew.

Notes

1. Worldometers.info.
2. The Center for the Study of Global Christianity (CSGC) at Gordon Conwell Theological Seminary, "Status of Global Christianity 2025," https://www.gordonconwell.edu/center-for-global-christianity/resources/status-of-global-christianity/.
3. Andrea Riccardi, *La Chiesa brucia: Crisi e futuro del cristianesimo*, (Bari-Rome: Laterza, 2021).
4. Quoted in Michael Plekon, *Living Icons: Persons of Faith in the Eastern Church* (University of Notre Dame Press, 2002), 234.
5. Several quotes in this book are taken from this interview, adapting the translation to the written edition. The interview, in Italian, can be found at https://www.raiplay.it/video/2025/05/Robert-Francis-Prevost-lintervista-esclusiva-prima-dellelezione-1f62f1be-933c-4446-b877-0407d93e4352.html.
6. Fr. Becket Franks, OSB, quoted in Michael Stechschulte, "Pope's Michigan High School Classmate Says He Was Smart, Well-liked, and 'Tutor' of the School," *OSV News*, https://www.osvnews.com/popes-michigan-high-school-classmate-says-he-was-smart-well-liked-and-tutor-of-the-school/.
7. Fr. Peter M. Donohue, quoted in Angela Barbuti, "Long before he was pope, Leo XIV was a skinny Villanova undergrad figuring out 'do you want to live this life,'" *New York Post*, May 10, 2025, https://nypost.com/2025/05/10/world-news/pope-leo-still-has-a-lot-of-love-for-his-alma-mater-villanova/?utm_campaign=nypost&utm_medium=referral.
8. Cardinal Robert Francis Prevost, interview with RAI.
9. Ibid.
10. Midwest Augustinians, "Foreign Missions," https://www.midwestaugustinians.org/foreign-missions.
11. *Annuario Pontificio 2001*, 1242.
12. "Biography of Pope Leo XIV, born Robert Francis Prevost," *Vatican News*, May 8, 2025, https://www.vaticannews.va/en/pope/news/2025-05/biography-of-robert-francis-prevost-pope-leo-xiv.html.
13. "L'ultima intervista del cardinale Prevost su Francesco," *Vatican News*,

May 8, 2025, https://www.vaticannews.va/it/papa/news/2025-05/papa-prevost-papa-francesco.html.

14. Ibid.

15. Letter of Pope Francis to the bishops of the United States of America, February 10, 2025, Vatican.va.

16. Hadeel Al-Shalchi, Anas Baba, and Daniel Estrin, "Palestinian deaths in Gaza rise above 50,000 as Israel expands its military campaign," *NPR*, March 23, 2025, https://www.npr.org/2025/03/23/nx-s1-5337938/palestinian-deaths-gaza-israel.

17. "Global fertility in 204 countries and territories, 1950–2021, with forecasts to 2100: a comprehensive demographic analysis for the Global Burden of Disease Study 2021," https://www.thelancet.com/journals/lancet/article/PIIS0140-6736(24)00550-6/fulltext.

18. Fifth Episcopal Conference of Latin America and the Caribbean, May 2007, see n. 44.

19. Marc Ouellet, "Was ist der Mensch? Christliche Anthropologie im Zeitalter des Pluralismus," *Communio*, January 19, 2024, https://www.herder.de/communio/theologie/christliche-anthropologie-im-zeitalter-des-pluralismus-was-ist-der-mensch/.

20. See "Health Disparities in Suicide," U.S. Centers for Disease Control and Prevention, https://www.cdc.gov/suicide/disparities/?CDC_AAref_Val=https://www.cdc.gov/suicide/facts/disparities-in-suicide.html.

21. CDC/NCHS National Vital Statistics System, "Provisional number of marriages and marriage rate: United States, 2000-2019," https://www.cdc.gov/nchs/data/dvs/national-marriage-divorce-rates-00-19.pdf.

22. "Religious 'Nones' in America: Who They Are and What They Believe," Pew Research Report, January 24, 2024, https://www.pewresearch.org/religion/2024/01/24/religious-nones-in-america-who-they-are-and-what-they-believe/.

23. "Watching Mass Online Remains Elevated Even With Mass Attendance Back to 2019 Levels," *1964*, March 12, 2025, https://nineteensixty-four.blogspot.com/.

24. *Deus Caritas Est*, December 25, 2005, n. 1.

25. Francis, *Fratelli Tutti*, October 3, 2020, n. 180

26. *Humanae Salutis*, December 25, 1961, n. 4.

27. Joseph Ratzinger, *Faith and the Future* (Ignatius Press, 2009).

28. Ratzinger's full address can be read at the website dedicated to Benedict XVI by Ignatius Press, https://www.benedictusxvi.com/fileadmin/benedictusxvi.de/startseite/Kirche-im-jahr-2000/what-will-the-church-look-like-in-2000.pdf.

29. Aid to the Church in Need, Religious Freedom Report, 2023, https://acninternational.org/religiousfreedomreport/reports/global/2023.

30. Aid to the Church in Need.

31. "'Footprints': Young people and religion, the results of an international survey presented in Rome," Pontifical University of the Holy Cross, https://en.pusc.it/article/young-people-results-international-survey.

32. Gregory A. Smith, Alan Cooperman, Becka A. Alper, Besheer Mohamed, Chip Rotolo, et al., Religious Landscape Study, Pew Research Center, February 26, 2025, https://www.pewresearch.org/religion/2025/02/26/religious-landscape-study-executive-summary/.

33. Augustine of Hippo, Sermon 121.

34. Augustine of Hippo, *Confessions*, I, 1.

35. Augustine of Hippo, *On the First Letter of John*, Homily 7.

36. Augustine of Hippo, Commentary on Psalm 144.

37. Andrea Tornielli, "Archbishop Prevost: ' The bishop is a pastor, not a manager,'" *Vatican News*, May 4, 2023, https://www.vaticannews.va/en/vatican-city/news/2023-05/archbishop-prevost-the-bishop-is-a-pastor-not-a-manager.html.

38. Homily delivered by Cardinal Robert F. Prevost on the feast of Saint Augustine, August 29, 2024, https://www.vaticannews.va/es/vaticano/news/2024-08/prevost-como-san-agustin-cultivemos-la-inquietud-del-corazon.html.

39. Ricardo Morales Jiménez, "Interview with Cardinal Robert Prevost OSA: 'Above all, a bishop must proclaim Jesus Christ,'" https://www.augustinianorder.org/post/interview-with-cardinal-robert-prevost-osa-above-all-a-bishop-must-proclaim-jesus-christ.

40. Homily delivered by Bishop Robert Prevost Martínez on the Feast of Corpus Christi 2020 – Chiclayo Cathedral, https://www.usat.edu.pe/articulos/homilia-de-mons-robert-prevost-martinez-por-la-fiesta-de-corpus

-christi-2020-catedral-de-chiclayo/.

41. Jiménez, "Interview with Cardinal Robert Prevost OSA."
42. Benedict XVI, *Deus Caritas Est*, n. 1.
43. Paul VI, *Evangelii Nuntiandi*, December 8, 1975, n. 41.
44. Tornielli, "Archbishop Prevost: 'The bishop is a pastor, not a manager.'"
45. Jiménez, "Interview with Cardinal Robert Prevost OSA."
46. "*L'ultima intervista del cardinale Prevost su Francesco*," *Vatican News*.
47. Speech by Bishop Robert Prevost at the Santo Toribio de Mogrovejo University in Chiclayo, October 14, 2015, https://www.latina.pe/entretenimiento/arriba-mi-gente/lo-mejor-amg/recuerda-el-discurso-robert-prevost-papa-leon-xiv-en-la-universidad-santo-toribio-de-mogrovejo-en-chiclayo_20250508/
48. Speech by Bishop Robert Prevost Martínez of Chiclayo and Grand Chancellor of the Catholic University of Santo Toribio de Mogrovejo, March 27, 2015, https://www.usat.edu.pe/discursos/discurso-de-mons-robert-prevost-martinez-obispo-de-chiclayo-y-gran-canciller-de-la-universidad-catolica-santo-toribio-de-mogrovejo-en-elmarco-de-la-presentacion-de-los-servicios-de-desarrollo-empre/.
49. Remarks by Bishop Roberto Prevost Martinez of Chiclayo during the first industrial forum of 2015, held at the Catholic University of Santo Toribio de Mogrovejo, May 29, 2015, https://www.usat.edu.pe/discursos/palabras-del-excelentismo-monsenor-roberto-prevost-martinez-obispo-de-chiclayo-y-gran-canciller-de-la-universidad-catolica-santo-toribio-de-mogrovejo-en-el-marco-del-i-foro-industrial-2015/.
50. Ibid.
51. Ibid.
52. Ibid.
53. Speech by Bishop Robert Prevost at the Santo Toribio de Mogrovejo University in Chiclayo, October 14, 2015.
54. Ibid.
55. Jiménez, "Interview with Cardinal Robert Prevost OSA."
56. Ibid.
57. Ibid.

About the Author

Jesús Colina is a journalist and publisher based in Rome. He is the former co-CEO and editorial director of Aleteia.org and CEO of Imedia.news. He was appointed by Pope Benedict XVI as consultant to the Pontifical Council for Social Communications (2008–16). Prior to that appointment, he served as CEO of H2Onews, a Catholic video agency for Catholic TV stations around the world. He is the former founder and CEO of Zenit.org and editorial director of the Digital Network of the Catholic Church Latin America. He holds a degree in philosophy from the Pontifical Gregorian University and in communication from the Complutense University of Madrid. He and his wife have three children.